A BO

GEORGEHAM

and the North West Corner of

DEVON

BY

LOIS LAMPLUGH

DESIGNED & ILLUSTRATED

BY

PETER ROTHWELL

1995

Westwell Publishing
Devon

Author's Acknowledgements

In writing this book I have once again been grateful for the facilities offered by the North Devon Athenaeum, the Local Studies Centre and the North Devon Record Office, whose staff have been unfailingly helpful.
I would like to thank John Breeds, Warden of Braunton Burrows Nature Reserve, for providing information concerning the present management of the Reserve.
I would also like to thank Peter Rothwell for his illustrations, which reflect his deep knowledge of and love for north Devon and enliven each chapter of the book.

Illustrator's Acknowledgements

The illustrator appreciates this opportunity to acknowledge his indebtedness to Sidney Jones, C.F. Tunnicliffe and John Dyke whose works have been a constant inspiration.

First published 1995 by Westwell Publishers
Friendship, Guineaford,
Barnstaple North Devon EX31 4EA

ISBN 0 - 9521413 - 2 - 9

Printed and bound by
The Lazarus Press
Bideford
Devon EX39 2EA

Ilfarcomb
L: noted for it's safe Har
bour for Shipping, for
y constant lights main
tain'd in it for y Direc:
tion of Sailors. And
for y Learned & judici
ous Mr. Camden's ha
ving been Prebenda:
ry of it, tho' a Layman
(at 44)

Chimleigh
Has a Mr. on The right
famous for y Preben:
said to have been found
ed here by y Lady of y
Manor for y Children,
n: w: she prevented the
Father from Drowning
as he designed, because
he had too many; and
for a Free School foun:
ded by G.D. of Bedford,
both w: have been —
sometime since des:
troyed. (at 44½) —

The BISHOPRICK of EXETER.
Contains the Counties of
Devon, & Cornwall,
& therein 604 Parish:
res, founded by K. Ed:
the Confessor, & Peter
Leofrick L: Chan:
celor first Bishop.
Value £500. —
See Exeter Palace, in

The DEANARY of EXETER.
Erected by William
Brewere, Bishop of
Exeter. A.D. 1225, first
Dean.

Chattel Hampton (at 91) Was the Kings De =
mesne at y Conquest, but has since been y Possession of
y E: of Glocester, Warwick, Bridgwater, & L.d Spencer
now belongs to Lewis Pollard.

(Lewis (at 89) Here was formerly an Alltar founded by Adeliza Daughter of
Baldwin of Oakhampton, A.o 1140. which produced two very famous men
in their times, Viz: Baldwin then Abbot & afterw:d Arch B.k of Canterbury in y
Reign of K. Rich:d: & Johannes Davrivis Confessor to K. John.

(Northam (at 57) This Manor was given by y Conqueror to St. Stephens in Caen, in Normandy the
Place is now famous for breeding Marriners & it's Steeple is a Sea Mark for Sailors.

A BOOK OF
GEORGEHAM
and the North West Corner of Devon
by
LOIS LAMPLUGH

DESIGNED & ILLUSTRATED
by
PETER ROTHWELL

About the Author

Lois Lamplugh grew up in the village of Georgeham. During the Second World War she served in the ATS and afterwards joined the editorial staff of Jonathan Cape. Following the birth of her second child she and her husband, Lawrence Carlile Davis – who is also a Devonian – moved back to the west country. During the 1970s Lois obtained an honour's degree from the Open University, and also taught for some years at a school for maladjusted boys.

She has written more than a dozen books for children, mostly for the older age group and with north Devon settings. Her books of local history include Barnstaple : Town on the Taw, A History of Ilfracombe, Minehead and Dunster, Take off from Chivenor and Lundy : Island without Equal. Her biography of Henry Williamson, A Shadowed Man, was published in 1990.

In the present book Lois traces the history of both the large parishes of Georgeham and the coast from the Taw-Torridge estuary to the Bristol Channel, and includes portraits of writers who lived in the area, from W.N.P. Barbellion to Henry Williamson.

About the Illustrator

Peter Rothwell was educated at Barnstaple Grammar School. He studied Art & Design at Dartington College of Arts and at The West of England College of Art in Bristol. Peter has four children and lives in the tiny hamlet of Goosewell near Berrynarbor in North Devon. He has spent all of his working life in the West Country. As well as working as a freelance designer in Bristol, Peter has taught in schools at Torquay, Axminster, and at Exeter University. For the last nine years Peter has been a Lecturer at North Devon College.

His work, both two and three dimensional, is regularly represented at exhibitions throughout the region.

A founder member of the Henry Williamson Society his work is well known to its members. He collaborated with Lois Lamplugh on her book *A Shadowed Man: Henry Williamson* and has had a collection of his drawings entitled *Lundy – An Island Sketchbook* published by Westwell Publishing.

Full List of Illustrations   Page Number

Contents

Page Number

1

From the Beginning

T he farthest north-west corner of Devon lies between the Taw-Torridge estuary and the Bristol Channel coast. It is about nine miles from north to south and four miles from east to west. Human occupation of the region may go back a long way – probably to some time in the Middle Stone Age, some five to ten thousand years ago. The first evidence to suggest this was discovered by an invalidish, reclusive man born in Torquay, Townsend Hall. A keen amateur geologist and archaeologist, he was exploring Baggy in 1863 in search of geological specimens when he came across a collection of worked flints – 366 in all. In 1920 Dr Thomas Young of Woolacombe, began a search of the area which produced a range of flint tools and tips for weapons – knives, scrapers, arrow heads, borers and so on. Perfect specimens of flint arrowheads have often been turned up by the plough on farmland on Baggy, which, in mesolithic times, when much of the North Atlantic was still clenched up in ice, resulting in considerably lower sea levels than those of today, could have been approached from the west over dry land. Other places, such as Spreacombe, Saunton Down, Woolacombe and Mortehoe have also yielded artefacts dated to this period, and collections of them are to be seen not only in the Museum of North Devon in Barnstaple but also in the Royal Albert Museum in Exeter and even in the Ashmolean in Oxford. People of slightly later times also left traces of their craftsmanship behind them: 'Flints of Neolithic and Bronze Age occur in animal disturbances and under ploughed conditions along the 500 foot crest of the hill (Saunton Down). These include one fine barbed and tanged arrowhead, a broken leaf-shaped arrowhead, a large number of scrapers and a retouched fragment of a polished axe.' Note 1

Later still Iron Age people, some of the Celts known as Dumnonii, seem to have made their homes in defended places not far from Georgeham. On the hill west of Spreacombe Manor is a horseshoe-shaped earthwork; west of Knowle a circular hill fort is marked on Ordnance maps as the Castle.

To visualize any familiar, peopled landscape as it may have been in prehistory is not easy. The imagination must erase every building, all roads and the vehicles that run on them, all hedges and boundary walls – even the grazing stock of the modern farmer – and picture a truly natural countryside, unencumbered by the enormous changes made by ever-increasing numbers of human beings in two thousand years or more. Along the coast, at least, much of the landscape was probably open downland; it seems unlikely that even during the Iron Age, when valleys may have been well wooded, trees could have withstood the strong Atlantic winds on the uplands – despite the fact that oak, ash, birch and hazel are known to have grown in parts of what is now Barnstaple Bay.

As far as is known, the Romans ignored much of Devon, contenting themselves with driving a road as far as the Celtic township they knew as Isca Dumnoniorum, which would become Exeter, and setting up signal stations at Old Barrow and Martinhoe to keep watch over the mouth of the river they called Sabrina, the Severn.

It may not have been until two centuries after the final withdrawal of the Roman legions from Britain that a few immigrant families began to settle north of the Taw. It has been suggested that Saxons did not reach Devon until around the middle of the 7th century, but that they then carried out a fairly rapid conquest covering fifty years, in three short bursts, c.660, 682 and 710, and that much of the occupation took the form of peaceful settlement rather than armed conflict.Note 2 It is at least known that there were some twenty Saxon manors in this remote corner of the country at the time of Duke William of Normandy's conquest in 1066. The remarkable survey taken twenty years later

2

names them and their owners who, like most of their kind, appear just once in history, and are gone: Fitell or Vitalis at Spreacombe, Eadmar or Etmar at North and South Hole and Georgeham, and so on. (Occasional variations in spelling are accounted for by the fact that, for the five western counties of England, there are two versions of Domesday: the Exchequer Book and the Exeter Book.) The relative size of manors is indicated by the area on which they had to pay geld, the land tax originated by the Saxon kings, discontinued in 1051 and revived by King William. The basis of geld assessments was the hide, a somewhat uncertain measure of area usually taken to be about 120 acres, subdivided into virgates (quarters) and ferlings (sixteenths).

In this part of Devon, as elsewhere, the distribution of manors among Norman lords – supposedly to prevent too great a concentration of power under a single lord in one area – seems somewhat haphazard. The king himself held Braunton. It paid tax on only one hide, but it was by far the richest and most populous manor in the area, valued at £16 a year by weight. Baldwin Fitzherbert de Meules, the king's deputy in Devon (Baldwin the Sheriff) had received Lincombe, taxed on two hides and worth £2 a year. The powerful and warlike Geoffrey de Mowbray, Bishop of Coutances, who had been granted extensive estates in Devon and Somerset, had Pickwell; Robert, Earl of Mortain, whose holdings spread across Cornwall, Devon, Somerset and Wiltshire, was granted Croyde, and a certain William Capra (Chievre or Cheever, the goat) had Woolacombe and North Buckland. It was a man called Tetbald, son of Berners, whose name is rendered by modern historians as Theobald Fitzberners, who held the largest group of manors in this small area north of Saunton (he had 27 manors in Devon altogether, and a house in Exeter).Note 3

Normans with scattered estates often sublet many of them, keeping just a few in their own hands. Theobald held Saunton, Spreacombe, North and South Hole and Georgeham himself, and sublet Ossaborough and Over Woolacombe. Saunton was the biggest of this little clutch of holdings; it was worth sixty shillings a year, which included thirty pence for its salt pan. Theobald's other manors were smaller still; North and South Hole were only taxed on half a virgate, and the others, apart from Georgeham, on one virgate. Ossaborough and Spreacombe had dropped in value since the Conquest – the former from fifteen shillings to five shillings and the latter from sixty

4

shillings to twenty shillings.

The population was very small by today's standards. It has been estimated that the whole county of Devon had only somewhere between sixty and eighty thousand people when the Domesday survey was taken, considerably less than the present population of Exeter.Note 4 Even Braunton had only four serfs, forty villeins and thirty bordars. If all these men were heads of families, with wives and two or three children, the total may have been no more than 350 people. Saunton had 24 working men and Croyde had 21. Georgeham had only seven – two serfs and seven villeins – so it is unlikely that there were more than three dozen people in this tiny settlement. Since it was not yet a parish, being included under Braunton until 1231, it is not permissable to include those who lived in places such as Croyde and Pickwell which are now within Georgeham parish.

In this thinly peopled landscape of tiny manors Saxons worked – no doubt resentfully – for their mostly absentee Norman masters. They cultivated crops; Domesday usually gives the number of ploughs that could be used. For instance, it was reported that there was land for ten ploughs in both Woolacombe and Croyde, and for six in both North Buckland and Georgeham. The Exeter Book gives details of stock, and so helps to fill out the picture of farming in 11th century Devon. Some Norman overseers may have encouraged the breeding of increased numbers of farm animals. Woolacombe had 300 sheep, five goats, twelve pigs and sixteen cattle. Croyde had 100 sheep, eleven oxen and twelve pigs; North Buckland had a cob (the only one reported for this area apart from Lincombe), 100 sheep, twenty goats, twelve cattle and five pigs. No animals are reported for Georgeham, however, and, surprisingly, the only animals reported for Pickwell are thirteen pigs. (The fact that sheep are set down to the nearest round figure suggests that the Norman clerks did not bother with exact numbers, and it is possible that they sometimes left out details of stock altogether.)

For nearly a century and a half after the Domesday survey was taken, Georgeham remained part of Braunton parish. It might have been expected that the Bishop of Coutances would order the building of a church on his manor of Pickwell, but evidently he did not. An undated manuscript survives from the time when Roger de Winkleghe was Dean of Exeter (1231-1252) which speaks of Robert de Edington as being both Patron and Parson of Hamme. A small church must therefore have been in existence at that time, but it may only just have been built. Evidence of 13th century construction is the piscina in the south wall of the Pickwell chapel, with its plain pointed arch, and a font discovered as recently as 1967 which has been dated to that century. Robert de Edington's successor, Oliver de Tracy, who became rector of Hamme in 1261, must have been related to the Henry de Tracy who was lord of Barnstaple for sixty-odd years of the 13th century. (An earlier Oliver de Tracy, a relation of an earlier Henry de Tracy of Barnstaple, allotted ten shillings a year to the monks of the Holy Saviour. The fact that this was payable at the time of Barnstaple Fair indicates the remarkable antiquity of this fair.)

The 13th century is also the time from which documents survive which give some idea of what had become of the Bishop of Coutances' holding of Pickwell. When he received it, it had twelve acres of meadow, 100 acres of pasture and paid geld for a modest half a hide. It was worked by a serf, four villeins and five bordars. The subtenant was a man called Drogo, who held many of the Bishop's lands from him. Worth five shillings at the conquest, it had doubled its value by 1086.

A man called Reinald was holding it in 1186, but not long afterwards it came into the hands of the St. Aubyn family, whose name was usually spelled St. Albino or Sancto Albino in the middle ages. There have been several saints called St. Aubyn, or St. Albinus. One of them, who died in 554, was bishop of Angers; an abbey was erected in his memory and is said to be still a popular place of pilgrimage. There are more than seventy places in France containing the name St. Aubyn, and it is not possible to know from which of them the first Mauger St. Aubyn came, or when. (According to one writer, there were four Maugers in five generations of the St. Aubyn family.)Note 5

The effigy of the one about whom most is known is still to be seen in Georgeham church. When he was born is a matter for conjecture, but the Inquisition Post Mortem taken after his death is dated 1294. (Inquisitions or enquiries such as these were held whenever a feudal tenant died, to establish and record the extent of his lands so that the king could exact the medieval equivalent of death duties.)

In 1249 this Sir Mauger granted 'the manor of Pidekwill and half a knight's fee in Hamme' to Robert de Pidikwill. Robert, having formally acknowledged in court that these holdings belonged to

6

Mauger, agreed to render one sore (year-old) sparrowhawk or two shillings at the feast of St. Peter's Chains (1st August) and all services with respect to them for life; after his death they were to revert to Sir Mauger and his heirs 'quit of the heirs of Robert for ever'.Note 6 Sir Mauger married Robert's daughter Isabel. They are known to have had at least four children: Joan, Isabel, Mauger and Guy. The dates of birth of three of them cannot be traced, but Mauger Junior must have been born in 1282, as he is said to have been twelve years old at the time of the Inquisition Post Mortem on his father.

Links between the two families were reinforced when, in 1261, Mauger agreed that Robert's other daughter, Idonea, and her husband Fulco Monsorel, should hold a tenement called Gratton, in High Bray, from himself and his heirs forever, 'rendering therefore as much foreign service as belongs to such a tenement of the same fee in the township in discharge of all services, customs and extaction'.Note 7

Records of transactions of this sort emphasize the strong hold of feudalism in medieval society: men did not own property, they held it in return for certain services, ultimately to the king. (A knight's fee was simply an obligation to provide military service to the Crown in the form of a fully armed and equipped knight, together with his retainers, for forty days each year. First introduced by Henry II in 1181, it was quite often commuted to the payment of scutage, a stipulated sum of money.)

Sir Mauger himself was called upon to fulfil his feudal duty in 1283. As Edward I was at that time in Wales putting down an insurrection led by Llewellyn and David ap Gryffyd, Sir Mauger would have been summoned to join his punitive expedition. One may imagine his riding out from wherever he was then living – perhaps Pickwell, if it had reverted to him by then – attended by men-at-arms, and making his way northwards to the Welsh border and beyond.

Sir Mauger seems to have been a rich man, and known to be willing to lend to the higher clergy: the Register of Bishop Walter Bronescombe of Exeter records a loan of fifty marks in 1258, while in 1282 his successor, Bishop Peter Quival, borrowed 100 marks. Sir Mauger was the patron of the living of Georgeham, and presented Sir Stephen Hayme to it in 1272. (Hayme, who had become Dean of Exeter in 1269, held other benefices, and almost certainly appointed a curate to minister to Georgeham.)

The 1294 enquiry noted that Sir Mauger had held the manors of

Hole and Hamme, as well as Pickwell; another document mentions additional holdings. At Pickwell he was a sub-tenant of Geoffrey de Camville, who had succeeded Henry de Tracy as lord of the manor of Barnstaple, having married de Tracy's daughter Matilda.

Sir Mauger's widow, Isabel, outlived him by at least 38 years, so was probably very young when she married. It would be interesting to know whether it was she, rather than Sir Mauger, who left instructions for their effigies to be sculpted and installed in the church. It has been said that they once lay side by side in front of the chancel arch, but hers, regrettably, was lost at some time, while that of her husband remained in its original position until the 19th century. The 17th century Devon antiquary Tristram Risdon, deduced from the size of his effigy that he was a man of great stature, but if his lady's was the same size, she would have been equally tall. Risdon repeated a legend of the knight's great strength, having been shown a huge stone he was supposed to have hurled a considerable distance.

It has been pointed out that Mauger Junior must have died without heirs by 1316, as Isabel succeeded to his estates and brought them to her husband Jordan de Haccombe. After Jordan's death in 1324 she married Sir Robert Cruwys; her estate then included 'Overhamme and their advowsons, and the moiety of the manor of Pidikwille'. Despite the mention of advowsons in the plural, it is clear that only one church existed.

Robert de Cruwys and Isabel made a grant to one of his relations in May 1332. Richard, 'son of Alexander de Cruwys, chivaler', took over Cruwys Morchard and various other holdings, as well as the rents in a dozen places, including Overhamme, Netherhamme, South Lobb and Ilfracombe. Moreover Richard was to have the advowsons of three churches, including Overhamme. Although he was granted half of the manor of Pickwell, 'Isabella, who was the wife of Mauger de Sancto Albino' – in other words Isabel de Cruwys's mother – was to hold in dower the other half.[Note 8] The age of the dowager Isabel, or Isabella, can only be guessed at. If she had been, say, twenty five when her son Mauger was born in 1282, she would have been about seventy five by this time. In this same year of 1332 Edward III raised a lay subsidy (clergy were exempt) and the list of fourteen taxpayers for Pickwell includes just one woman – Isabel de Sancto Albino. Like her son-in-law Robert de Cruwys, she had to pay twelve pence.[Note 9]

Documents such as these indicate that for much of the 13th and early 14th centuries Pickwell was of much greater importance than Georgeham, and must have been the site of a manor house owned by the St Aubyn family – in which, it may be imagined the widowed Isabel St Aubyn lived out her days. Remarkably, Georgeham does not appear in the 1332 tax lists, despite the fact that it had evidently possessed its parish church for some hundred years. The list for Cridho, or Croyde, shows a total of 28 men having as little as eightpence, though the lord of the manor, Baldwin Flemyng, was charged five shillings. Two men, Thomas Gryffyrd and William Gauntel, appear twice in the list, so evidently had two tenements; two others must have lived at what is now Forda, as their names are given as Mauger atte Forde and Walter atte Forde.

Isabel de Cruwys had only one child, Cecilia, the daughter of her first husband, Jordan de Haccombe. Cecilia married Sir John Lercedekne. He was a member of a family which held a large estate in Cornwall. (Its surname was in fact Archdeacon, but it appears in medieval documents in a remarkable number of varied spellings.) Sir John, a Knight of the Shire, was M.P. for Cornwall in 1332 and 1336. He fought in the French wars, but while in England lived mostly at Lanihorn. In 1365 he and Cecilia came to an agreement with an Adam de Pistre concerning a wide range of properties in Devon and Cornwall, including Lobb, Churchill in East Down, Pickwell, Overhamme and Netherhamme. 'They acknowledged the tenements to be the right of Adam as by their gift. For this Adam granted them to John and Cecilia and gave them up to them at the court. To have and to hold to John and Cecilia during their lives of the chief lords of that fee by the services which belong to the said tenements'. After their deaths these lands were to descend to Sir John's heirs.

Sir John was the patron of several benefices, including Georgeham, and in 1361, with Cecilia and her aunt Joan, née St Aubyn, who was the widow of a Thomas de Mertone, he presented Andrew de Tregors to 'Sancti Georgii de Hamme'.

Sir John died in 1337. He had fathered nine sons; the eldest predeceased him; the second, Warin, became his heir and lord of Pickwell and other places. The name of his seventh son was Martin. It seems probable that the Martin Lercedykene who became rector of Georgeham in 1422 was a son or grandson of this seventh son.[Note 10]

During the next hundred years the manor of Pickwell, and with it the advowson of Georgeham, passed to members of the Talbot and

9

Carew families. Although those who succeeded them – the Newcourts and the Harrises – seemed to have maintained considerable local status, Pickwell had lost its former dominance. The parish of Georgeham, including North Buckland, Darracott, Putsborough and Croyde, as well as Pickwell, had taken its place as the heart of the far north west corner of Devon.

GEORCEHAM.

2

The Growing Village.

℘here is no way of knowing how villages such as Georgeham were affected by the outbreak of bubonic plague, known as the Black Death, which reached the coast of Dorset in 1348 and spread rapidly across the country. If the parson of a parish was replaced in the late 1340s, it may indicate that he was a victim, and therefore that many of his parishioners were also, but the fact offers no certainty. In Georgeham, although Master William de Doune was followed by Master John de Dyrworthe in 1349, it is possible that he died of other causes than plague, or moved to another parish. (Dyrworthe's successor, Sir Andrew de Tregors, remained as rector of Georgeham until 1374).

In England in general, numbers increased gradually once the last of the epidemics (there were four altogether during the 14th century) had subsided. However, when Henry VIII began to raise taxes for his war with France in 1524, the population of what, by that time, is set down as Georgeham parish, may have been much the same as it had been when Edward III had demanded his lay subsidy in 1332. This time people were taxed on the basis of land, goods or wages. In Georgeham, which would now have included such places as Croyde and Pickwell, formerly listed separately, 77 people paid on goods, and just one, John Mayne, paid on land. The fact that no one was assessed on wages suggests that there were quite a few workers – almost certainly those who laboured on farms – who were too poorly paid to be taxed at all. However, the goods on which tax was levied might include coin, plate, stock of merchandise, harvested corn and household chattels, so the 76 people assessed must have been reasonably well off for that period.

Towards the end of his reign, Henry taxed his people once more; in 1543-5 the number assessed in Georgeham had gone up to 89, and this time the names of twelve women, mostly widows, appear. In Mortehoe, which had 48 taxpayers, five women had to pay, though one woman, Joan Blackmore, appears in Georgeham also, so either two women shared the same name, or one owned two properties.[Note 1]

In 1538 Thomas Cromwell, Henry VIII's Vicar General, decreed that parishes should begin to keep registers of baptisms, marriages and burials. Many places seem to have made no effort to comply for some twenty or thirty years, or even longer, but Georgeham was obedient. Its register of marriages and burials began promptly in 1538, though for some reason baptisms were left until two years later. At this time the living of Georgeham was held by John Holway, Canon of Exeter, and although he must have been a pluralist, he probably made sure that a curate in Georgeham began keeping records. The original registers were on paper, but in 1692 Thomas Macye, curate to the long-lived rector William Culme, who died in 1638 aged 90, copied them on to parchment to ensure their preservation.

From 1538 to 1625, most years show more baptisms than burials – anything from three to fourteen or fifteen more – so there must have been a steady rise in the population. Even in 1571, when 27 people died because, the register notes, 'the plague was in Ham', there were eighteen baptisms, and for many years before and after this epidemic births usually considerably outnumbered deaths.

Henry VIII's wars with France aroused fears of invasion. To prepare a sort of Tudor Home Guard he directed that every parish should list all the men between the ages of sixteen and sixty who were fit to fight, and that all who could afford it should pay for weapons and armour. Assessments were made on the basis of land or goods; those who were too poor to be assessed individually ('those not charged according to the statute') had to contribute towards a stipulated amount of armour and weapons.

Elizabeth I continued these preparations, although Spain, rather than

France, became the potential invader. In 1569, across England, muster rolls were prepared, and local men of good standing were sworn in as 'presenters'. The presenters sworn for Georgeham were John Swete and William Borowe or Borough. 'John Newcourt, gent.', in other words the John Newcourt who brought Pickwell from Sir Peter Carew in 1560, heads the list; other men who had to provide weapons or certain items of armour were John Cutlief, James Talbot, Thomas Peren and the presenter, William Borough.

The poorer inhabitants had to contribute towards the cost of two corselets, two pikes, two calivers and two murrions. The 'able men' included ten archers, four harquebusiers, nine pikemen and two billmen.

In Mortehoe the poorer people had to find only one each of the armour and weapons listed above; there were four archers, seven harquebusiers, three pikemen and six billmen, confirming the smaller population of Mortehoe parish indicated by the 1543-5 tax lists.[Note 2]

The general upward trend of population in Georgeham, with births exceeding deaths year by year, continued into the 1620s, but for the rest of the 17th century the reverse was the case. Nevertheless, by the beginning of the 1640s, there may have been as many as six or seven hundred people in the parish of Georgeham. The document that suggests this is the list of those who signed the Protestation returns. Following considerable unrest among members of parliament during the passage of the bill for the attainder of the Earl of Strafford in 1641, ten members were appointed to draw up a document which required all signatories to 'vow and protest' that they would maintain the Protestant religion, defend the king and the privileges of parliament, oppose all plots and conspiracies and 'endeavour to preserve the Union' (of England, Scotland and Ireland). There is irony in the fact that a large number of those who signed copies of this document when they were distributed countrywide would, within a few years, be fighting against the king to whom they were pledging their fealty.

In Georgeham, 211 people signed, including the rector, John Berry, the constable, George Sweete, two churchwardens – John Harry and Edmund Ellott (so spelled) – and two overseers, John Tooker and Nicholas Harper. All who signed were men so, if each had a wife and no more than one child, the total would exceed 600.[Note 3]

It does not seem that the Georgeham area was much affected by the

13

Civil War. Commanders on the opposing sides were more interested in holding towns, naturally enough; villages such as those north of Saunton, not on a main route likely to be used by detachments of either army, were fairly safe from pillage or occupation. The parish registers were kept throughout the period of the war, which was certainly not the case everywhere.

After the Restoration, Charles II looked about for ways to raise money. In 1667 he introduced a hearth tax. In every parish, returns listed those who were liable for tax and, as usual, those who were too poor to pay – many of them with a single hearth in, probably, a one up and one down cottage. These returns can often be useful to indicate the size of a 17th century village and the number of substantial houses it contained. Unfortunately the document concerning Georgeham is badly mutilated, with parts of names or numbers of hearths illegible: only 48 names survive, but many more have been lost.

In 1667 the house with the most hearths was owned by William Newcourt, who was accorded 'Esq.' after his name. He had eleven. It is impossible to know where his house stood, but it seems unlikely that it was Pickwell, which in the second half of the 17th century was owned by members of the Harris family. Thomas Colley, the rector, had nine hearths, so the rectory must have been a fair-sized house even then.Note 4

At this time what were known as briefs were issued authorising the collection in churches of funds to help rebuild places that had suffered damage by fire or storm. Between 1660 and 1672, Georgeham parish registers record six collections of this kind: the quays at Combwich and Watchet needed repair, and in places as far away as Marlborough and Kingston-on-Thames, people had suffered as a result of fires.

One exciting event was noted in the register for 1680. 'The great blazing Star or Comet appeared on December 14th and continued to the end of Jan. Visible to us heer'. The transcriber of the registers, W. R. Rogers, added a note 'This was Halley's Comet'. However, this is an error. The comet of 1680 was a completely different astronomical event, important in that it provided Newton with the opportunity to make repeated observations, as a result of which he developed a technique for determining the parabolic orbit of a comet. Edmond Halley, then aged 24, was in Paris at the beginning of a Continental tour; he also studied the comet with interest, but the one to which his name would be attached made one of its periodic appearances in

1682. His researches and calculations concerning this led him to publish, in 1705, the prediction that it would reappear in 1758 or early 1759. However, when it did so, Halley had been dead for sixteen years.[Note 5]

3

Questions about the Parish

The answers to two questionnaires sent out to Devon parishes in the 18th century provide details that help to give some idea of what life was like in villages of the time. The first, issued by the Dean of Exeter in 1727, asked every parson in the diocese to complete a terrier, or report, on his church and its lands, including the nature of the tithes. The rector of Georgeham in that year was the Revd Carew Hoblyn, who had been instituted in 1698, and was to die in 1728. He reported that Georgeham rectory was 'a Dwelling house built and covered with stone'. Its hall had an earthen floor, but there was a parlour floored with board and wainscotted, a little parlour also floored with board and wainscotted, and a kitchen floored with stone. There were also a dining room, a pantry and three cellars, a study, a closet and 'Seven Chambers three hung and four with white walls'. These would have been the bedrooms; those with hangings were probably for the parson's family, while the whitewashed ones would have been for servants. Out houses were built of stone and mud walls (cob, presumably), thatched with reed. A dairy, a brew house, stables, barns (one near the house and the other in Croyde), a shippon, a straw house and a dovecote completed the extensive establishment of this 18th century country parson. He also had the Home Stall, which consisted of 'two little orchards both of

them a quarter of acre and two gardens all bounded with the land of Wright.

Glebe land extended to just over 33 acres in all, scattered around the outskirts of the village. Each was enclosed and its boundaries identified by the properties it adjoined: the Pittis, for instance, was 'about four acres Bounded with the Manor lands and the land of John Harris Esq.' John Harris, who had married Dorothy Hancock, the (adopted daughter of Jane née Newcourt) and Gregory Chichester in 1673, died in the year the Dean's questionnaire was issued. (His grandson, another John, who had been born in 1703, became M.P. for Barnstaple with Henry Rolle, later Baron Rolle, in 1741, and represented the borough again in 1754, this time with George Amyard.)

The church plate consisted of a communion cup and cover weighing 21 ounces, inscribed with the Richards arms, a silver paten weighing 11½ ounces, a pewter plate and two pewter flagons.

Tithes were mostly payable in kind 'except the Usage of paying Three shillings and fourpence for the Manor mills and Two shillings each Per Annum for the two Mills'. One mill was at Croyde, another, Hole Mill, stood in a meadow a short distance west of Forda. (There was a third mill at Heddon but this may have been excluded from the survey.)

Other payments were a penny for the milk of a cow, sixpence for a calf, a farthing for the milk of a ewe, and a penny for a herb garden. If anyone had seven lambs, the rector usually had one, 'allowing the parishioners threepence for each number above that'. If under seven the rector is paid threepence for each Number below that'. As the literal meaning of tithes was a tenth, not a seventh, Georgeham's rector seems to have been exceeding his rights.

As far as fees were concerned, 'for Marriage usually one shilling, for churching usually sixpence, for Burial nothing but Mortuaries are paid'.

The parish clerk's salary was 'Sixteen shillings in Moneys four pence of every housekeeper', which seems to mean that a number of householders, rather than housekeepers in the modern sense, contributed to his salary; sixteen shillings, or 192 pence, divided by four would mean that 48 'housekeepers' helped to make up the total.

The sexton received a modest eight shillings. Both were appointed by the rector.

The document was signed by the Revd Hoblyn, John Harris of Pickwell, two churchwardens, two overseers and nineteen other men, two of whom were only able to make their mark.

The second request for information about Devon parishes came from the Revd Jeremiah Milles, Precentor (and later Dean) of Exeter Cathedral. Intending to write a history of the county, he prepared a long list of questions – over a hundred – and sent them out, on printed forms, to all the parochial clergy in the diocese. Not all replied, and some returned the form saying that they had no information, but it seems that the majority made an attempt to answer at least some questions; Dr Milles had 'only requested that the gentlemen will be so kind as to answer such questions as they have any knowledge of, leaving those unanswered of which they are entirely uncertain, and writing No or None to such of them as furnish no other answer'.

The forms are said to have been sent out about 1755-56. At that time the Revd William Chichester was rector of Georgeham, but he did not deal with his copy of the questionnaire himself; he handed it over to a Revd Wright, a school teacher in Barnstaple – possibly a relation of the landowner named Wright whose property adjoined the glebe lands in 1727.

He answered 'No' to a good many of the questions. However, asked the length and breadth of the parish according to the points of the compass he wrote 'By Braunton to ye South and East and partly by West Down by Mortehoe in the North, Severn Sea to ye West'. Disappointingly, he did not answer a question as to the number of houses in the parish, but recorded that Ham town was in the middle of it, the villages of Putsborough, Croyde and Cross to the west, and Darracott to the east. George Buck, Esq., was lord of the manor of Ham and Buckland; the manor was 'dismembered among John Harris Esq., Philip Webber, Gent., and Mr Joseph Baller and Smith, Esq. The church was 'in Mr Buck's manor and in the middle of the parish'; the tower was 70 feet high, had six bells and the patron was Sir John Chichester. (Sir John ceased to be patron in 1782.) Enquiries about its form and sizes, building materials, memorials or inscriptions of coats of arms carved or painted in the windows received the answer 'No', as did others concerning Roman or Danish remains, obelisks, standing stones, ancient castles, rare or uncommon plants and other things. There was a gentlemen's seat at Pickwell (spelled Piddeswell), owned by John Harris, there was a ruined chapel at Croyde said to be dedicated to St. Helen, and another at Buckland dedicated to St. Anthony. Although there was no marble, limestone, brick clay or other such materials, and no 'impression of land or sea animals or shells found in quarries', Mr Harris had 'an excellent quarry of Blue stone that will bear a chizzel as well as freestone'.

To the question, 'What Wakes, Parish Feasts or Processions?' Mr Wright replied simply 'Wake after St. George's Day'. This was evidently what came to be known as Ham Revel, the celebration of St. George's Day, April 23rd, the patronal festival of the church. 'Wake' in this sense is an old word for this sort of jollification, which usually included sports and dancing; it lingered in the north of England in the tradition of Wakes Week.

Mr Wright provided some useful information in answer to questions about agriculture in the parish. The land was 'more hilly than level, mostly enclosed', with soil that was part sand and part 'malmy'. There were about eleven acres of meadow, worth thirty shillings. Pasture was worth from from five to twenty shillings. Wheat, barley and oats were grown, and the land was manured with sand and dung. About 100 hogsheads of 'middling sweet' cider were made yearly; it was worth ten shillings a hogshead. There were about twenty acres of woodland – oak, ash and elm, mostly coppice. Cattle were black, sold at Barnstaple, Fremington and South Molton markets. In answer to the question, 'Are they remarkable for their size, shape, colour or breed?' Mr Wright answered stoutly. 'Handsome all.' (Robert Fraser, writing his *General View of the County of Devon* in 1794, said. 'The breed of cattle in the North of Devon is remarkably fine, and are. perhaps, the best in the kingdom'.) As far as climate was concerned, the air was sharp and dry, reputedly wholesome: a surprising judgement, to anyone used to the sea mists, drizzles and downpours of this part of the country.

In view of the fact that Dr Milles' questionnaire is thought to have been sent out in the mid-1750s, it is puzzling that Mr Wright reported that the church has six bells, since the sixth was cast for John Richards in 1765. Mr Richards was a benefactor to the parish. Not only did he give a bell, and join with the Revd Chichester in adding a flagon to the church plate, but he left five pounds in his will, in the form of a rent charge on two properties owned in Croyde, so that schooling could be provided for poor children. The Revd Thomas Hole, who became rector of Georgeham in 1783, bought the properties,and arranged for the five pounds to be paid as part of the salaries of two schoolmistresses, one in Georgeham and the other in Croyde.

Thomas Hole began an association of the Hole family with Georgeham parish which was to last a remarkably long time. Members of the family were patrons of the living from 1783 until 1886, and no fewer than five were rectors: Thomas Hole himself, 1783-1831, his son Francis, 1831-1866, the two generations thus completing an unbroken period of 83 years, a second Thomas Hole for a single year,1869, a second Francis Hole, 1870-1871, and finally William Henry George Francis Hole, 1886-1914.

It would be interesting to know whether the last celebration of Ham Revel took place during the time of W.H.G.F. Hole. If so, it was probably a less vigorous, and even violent, event than those in earlier days. Describing a village fête held in the glebe field in 1924, in aid of a new bell-cage for the church tower, Henry Williamson quoted an old man as saying, 'I mind the time when old Pas'n Hole held the Ham Revel in thaccy glebe field.' If this old man was in his seventies, and was speaking of his early childhood, he would have been looking back to some time in the 1850s, when the first Francis Hole was rector. The revel then included such traditional things as climbing a greasy pole, guessing the weight of a pig and skittling to win a pig – but there was also badger baiting, using terriers, and wrestling. A man whom Henry Williamson calls Sparker Ley, aged 94 in 1924, was the champion wrestler of the district as a young man. In church on the Sunday before the revel he would 'put his beaver hat firmly on his head and walk slowly up the aisle to the pulpit, and back again. This was the yearly challenge with the silver spoons won at previous revels stuck in the brim of his hat'.

In *The Patchwork Quilt*, one of the six stories that make up H.C. O'Neill's *Devonshire Idylls*, first published about 1892, the narrator gives an account of wrestling in a Devon village on the edge of Dartmoor in the mid-19th century. 'Squire Chanter, he's give them a silver spoon to wrestle for. 'Twas Revel Sunday, you know, miss; and it always used to be the manner to stick the prize up in front of the gallery, where all the lads could see un. the man-folk were all wild to try their strength. And the parson, he said, "Let 'em wrestle, if they've a mind to, and good luck to their backs. I wish I was young myself." That's what he said. And I think he was right, I do. So long as they catch hold fair, and don't wear naily boots, I sem it's a Christian play, just so well as that there cricketing parson nowaday tell so much about.'

But according to the account given in Williamson's *The Village Book*. Georgeham's wrestlers not only wore 'naily boots' but went to the blacksmith to have 'iron hacking caps with edges like plough coulters hammered to the fronts of their boots', and the kicking of opponents' shins with these iron toecaps was not only permitted, but apparently expected. Before the contest began each man threw down his hat and was given a pint of beer brewed in the rectory; the parson then chose the first two combatants by kicking over two hats at random.

Mr Hole, like many of his contemporary parsons, was a hunting man. Sparker used to feed his hounds, 'a mixed and savage pack which was kennelled in a small stone shed with a hayling roof in the meadow now called Kennel Field'.

The parson was a clerical martinet of whom the villagers were wary. He carried 'a long coach whip, with which he flicked at leaves and sticks and stones.' He could use it with such accuracy that he had been known to kill a goldfinch with one flick. He was not, in other words, a genial or compassionate man, always assuming that this portrait, seen at two removes, has not been darkened for dramatic effect.[Note 1]

4

In Touch with Fashion

It might be thought that in the mid-18th century, Georgeham was simply a remote village completely out of touch with London life, and that any woman living there – even if she was of the leisured middle class – would have found it difficult to learn anything of the latest songs, dances, games and fashions in clothes unless she or some of her family were in the habit of visiting the capital.

But a small vellum-bound volume, measuring just five by three inches, in the possession of the North Devon Athenaeum, shows that publications existed which could supply information to keep even the most provincial lady up to date.

The little book was published for the year 1764. Pages for entering 'memorandums (sic), observations, appointments and personal accounts' for the first five months are missing, and almost all the rest are regrettably blank. The only diary-type entry may provide a clue to the original owner: 'Left Georgeham December 27th to Youlston'. Youlston had been the home of one branch of the Chichester family since the 13th century. Sir John Chichester was living there at this time. As has been said, he was patron of the living of Georgeham, and had presented his younger brother William to it in 1750.**Note 1** William

Chichester and his wife Mary had four children – Francis, Anne, John and Elizabeth. They were left motherless by the death of Mary Chichester in September, 1760, when Elizabeth was only three years old. By 1764 Anne would have been 13. Did some indulgent relation give her the pocketbook as a Christmas present, and did she travel to Youlston two years later to stay with her uncle and his family? Or did the book belong to a member of the household in Georgeham rectory – a children's nurse or governess – whose duties may have included accompanying the young Chichesters on a visit?

There seems no doubt that the vellum binding of the book (which had a clasp, now broken) is the reason for its survival after nearly two and a half centuries. It may never have left Georgeham until it was deposited with the North Devon Athenaeum. On the flyleaf is scrawled 'Peter Clibbett, his pokket (sic) book, his hand and pen God Bless King George and all his men'. There are a number of Clibbetts (sometimes spelled Clibbet or Clebbet) in the Georgeham parish registers. A Peter whose surname is spelled Clebbet was born in 1748 and so would have been sixteen in 1764, though the book may not have come into his hands until some years later. (He married an Esther Thomas in 1776.) Yet another claimant of the book wrote, near the end 'Thomas Lake His Book November 21st 1799.' One page contains notes of expenses for board and lodgings for three days in January, 1801 (dinner at some inn called the Swan cost 3s 6d, lodging and breakfast cost three shillings, and a fee of two shillings was paid for a 'Bill of Inditment' (sic), which suggests that Thomas was a lawyer's clerk.

Since the 17th century, several rectors and their wives had been buried in the chancel of Georgeham church (John Berry, 1649; Thomas Colley, 1698, and his wife Mary; Carew Hoblyn, 1728, and his wife Catharine, 1725) but when the Revd William Chichester's wife Mary died at the age of thirty-three, a vault was constructed. This became the burial place of a number of members of the Chichester family, including Mr Chichester himself, who died ten years after his wife at the early age of forty-eight. His daughter Anne had an even shorter life than her mother. She married the Revd Thomas Hole, the first of his family to be rector of Georgeham, and had one child, William, who died in infancy in July, 1779; she herself died in December the following year at the age of 29. (The Revd Thomas remarried, and he and his second wife, Elizabeth, had three sons,

William, Francis and Robert, and twins, Henry and Mary. Francis was in due course to become his father's curate, and succeed him as rector, as has been said. Robert also entered the church; he died in 1843 at the age of 42.)

Anne Hole is touchingly described on a memorial tablet in the chancel as 'Early, Bright, Transient, Chaste, as morning dew she sparkled and exhal'd and went to Heaven. Few years but yield us proof, of Death's Ambition to cull his victims from the fairest field and sheath his shafts in all the Pride of Life'.

Whether or not the 'Lady's Pocketbook for the Year 1764' first belonged to her, its contents fascinate. Like a woman's magazine of today, it includes beauty hints, advice on health, recipes, fashion notes (with a full-length drawing of 'a Lady in the Dress of the Year 1763' and 'A Lady in the Riding Dress of the Year 1763') and details of the latest popular songs.

Recipes varied considerably. 'Dr Barry's Receipt for making the Beef-Tea: an admirable Strengthening Drink for all Weak Constitutions' and a broth of mutton knuckle bones ('an admirable restorative for weak or decayed constitutions') contrast with an Everlasting Syllabub which made lavish use of cream, sugar, wine and eggs, and also a Grand Trifle. The latter contained gelatin (homemade, necessarily, at a time when no shop-bought product was available) and was apparently made up of layers of matrimony cakes (currants sandwiched between two pastry cases) and Naples biscuits, which were made of flour, breadcrumbs, sugar, milk and whites of egg. The whole thing was covered in cream, raspberry jam and currant jelly. Rather less rich recipes were for rhubarb tart, plum cake, lemon cake, plain custard and three kinds of syrup, of marsh-mallow, violets and corn poppies. (The last-named must have been used as a sleeping draught.)

There were tips for preserving fruit. Bottled gooseberries, their stoppers sealed with resin, could be buried in the earth; this was said to keep them better than simply storing them in a dry place. Apricots, peaches, nectarines, cherries and 'plumbs' would keep well in layers of dry sand, 'so you will have them fit for tarts or other uses, till the next season'. Grapes might be preserved on the vine, each bunch protected by a bag of oiled white paper.

An 'eminent physician' was well aware of the psychosomatic origins of many illnesses: he listed some of the emotions to be avoided by

those who wanted to stay healthy, such as fear, grief, envy, hatred, malice, revenge and despair. He warned that these were known to 'weaken the nerves, retard the circulation, hinder perspiration, impair digestion and produce spasms, obstructions and hypochondriacal disorders.' Moreover 'intemperance, ignorance and indolence not only shorten and embitter our days, but hasten the death of the natural. Few attain to that period which Nature designed; vapours and spleen are too often our own acquisition and destruction'. Men lived in one round of sloth, he complained; was it any wonder that such men 'should fall into stone, gravel, gout, palsy, apoplexy' and other such diseases? Tea drinking would be beneficial if it was confined to people 'of rigid fibre and active lives', especially as it was usually drunk with sugar, which had 'a saponaceous antiseptic property', but all too often it was the indulgence of the lazy and indolent, of weak nerves and relaxed fibres, and the result was indigestion, sickness, fainting, tremors, flatulence and vapours. The eminent physician had evidently developed a wholly disillusioned view of his self-indulgent leisured patients. He contrasts them with the weary labourer who made a happy meal on brown bread, sprouts and bacon, and after sound sleep rose stout and ready for the next day's labour.

A 'Lady of Distinction' gave advice in the form of a letter to a mother who wanted to improve the 'personal charms' of her daughter. She tantalized her readers by offering to tell them the secret of a 'never failing beauty wash', which turned out to be no more than washing in 'fair water' and abstaining from 'sudden gusts of passion, particularly envy, as that gives the skin a sallow paleness'. The girl was to exercise temperance in eating and drinking 'to avoid those pimples, for which the advertised washes are a boasted cure'; she was to cultivate 'ingenious candour and unaffected good humour', get up early and avoid late hours, and card-playing, the latter being 'the mother of wrinkles'. In other words there was no magic beauty wash, but only the old, old maxim, so boring to the young and many of the not so young: moderation in all things.

Those who did play cards were by now favouring a game called quadrille, played by four people, using a pack of only forty cards, the eight, nines and tens being discarded. It sounds a complicated game; like ombre, which it superseded, it originated in Spain, and most of the terms were Spanish. There were games in red and games in black. The penalty for playing the 'vole', whatever that was, and failing to win three tricks, sounds uncomfortable: a player who did so was 'basted alone, unless he played forced spadille'.

Whist, originally a game for the lower classes, had become fashionable. Detailed directions for playing it are provided, as well as 'new laws of whist, as established at White's and Sanders's Chocolate Houses.'

The dance called quadrille was to remain popular for many years, but the pocketbook provided descriptions of 'twelve new country dances for the year 1764'. One has the same title as a successful play of the time, *Love in a Village;* among others are *Sweethearts in Plenty, The Prince of Wales's Birthday, Live in Clover* and *Trip to the World's End.* The instructions for dancing each one are brief, and give the impression that it was difficult to introduce much variety into the basic patterns of the country dance.

The words of 'the favourite new songs, sung in the year 1763 at Ranelagh House, Vauxhall and Marybone (sic) Gardens, and other polite concerts, both public and private' are given, but the music could not, of course, be included.

The rules of etiquette which held Victorian society in a grip as the restricting as the whalebone corsets worn by its fashionable women had not developed in the 18th century. Yet the pocketbook contains a striking reminder that what it called 'Ceremony' was not merely a social matter: it had political implications, helping to ensure that everyone stayed in what was regarded as their proper places, and did not start to get above themselves. It had the effect of marking out 'the bounds of high and low life' and distinguished 'all the intermediate spaces'. If 'place and power, birth and figure, were not to be adorned with ceremony and pomp, 'tis probable the vulgar would lose their distance, and by looking boldly into the merits of their superiors, break down the barriers at once, and set the world on a level'. A more damning indictment of the sham 'superiority' of the contemporary high life could hardly have been written.

Two simple sentences make all that has gone before superfluous. 'Good manners are founded on this single rule: to bear the frailties of others, and take care that our own shall not offend. If we add a grace in doing trifles, and ease in the affairs of the moment, we finish the gentleman or lady at once, and ceremony can add no more'.

One of the new country dances described in the book was called 'Love and Friendship'. This seems to have been a popular phrase in the late 18th century, and it appears as the subject of an exchange of letters between Theodore, apparently a bachelor, and Theodora, who is said to be the mother of fine children. Theodora begins by reproaching Theodore for sending her "the epistle now before me, the greater part of which is in a style equally improper for you to write, or me to read . . . For instance, I must insist on the banishment of the word 'love'". However, she adds that "by love I mean no guilty passion, no criminal desire which debases human nature, but the most exalted esteem and regard, founded in reason and virtue". Theodore protests at some length that there is no danger of his plunging into 'the miseries of an irregular passion'. They go on in this way for some time, until Theodore has the last word by declaring, "In short, madam, two words give us to understand what each other means. Your friendship was friendship simple and alone; my love was love and friendship together, and that you acknowledge to be a state of the most supreme satisfaction".

The fact that the phrase 'Love and Friendship' was still much in use towards the end of the century is shown by a piece of light-hearted satire written in 1790 by a girl of fifteen, also in the form of letters. Making exuberant fun of the absurdities to be found in many popular novels of the time, it was read aloud to amuse the writer's family. The writer was Jane Austen, and she called her parody 'Love and Friendship' (her slight mis-spelling, 'Love and Freindship' has always been retained). In her mature novels, of course, her heroines sought always to marry for love, but did so in a provincial society where marriage might all too often be arranged for materialistic reasons. With this in mind, it is amusing to find, written in an adult hand inside the back cover of the pocketbook, 'Captain Smith is going to be married to a woman with five or six thousand pounds fortune'. This adds a final enigmatic touch to the puzzle of the book's ownership.

5

The Worst Wreck on the Coast

ntries in Georgeham's burial registers sometimes provide reminders that this village, sheltered in its inland hollow, lay near a dangerous coast. The bodies of sailors drowned nearby were sometimes brought to the churchyard for burial. A shipwreck in 1600 resulted in the recovery of ten bodies; after another in 1608, six were found. Two men were drowned at Croyde in 1783, and between 1824 and 1844 the register records eight burials of men (or in one case a man and a woman) 'washed in on the sands' or 'on Croyde sands'.

It is surprising that there were not more drownings. According to Richard Larn, the bay between Baggy and Morte Point was feared by ship masters in the days of sail even more than Hartland Point, and without question 'dozens of 16th and 17th century wrecks took place there . . . but only details of the scow *Charfield*, stranded on Woolacombe sands in 1719, have been passed down to the present day'.[Note 1] In 1771 *Diana*, a brigantine from Boston carrying timber, was lost on Pickwell sands, in other words Putsborough. But the wreck which became the most widely known, and made the most impression on the minds of people living in north Devon, was of a naval vessel.

Early in 1799 *H.M.S. Weazle,* referred to as a sloop or brig, commanded by the Hon. Henry Grey, son of the Earl of Stamford, had been stationed at Appledore for some time. It was known that large quantities of spirits were being landed secretly along the north Devon coast – favourite places were Lee, Mortehoe and Watermouth – and the *Weazle* had been on preventive duty, patrolling along the English and Bristol Channels in search of smugglers. According to a contributor to a Barnstaple magazine published in 1824, her whole company was well known to local people, among whom 'their gaiety and social character seems to have become proverbial' – so much so that it was later rumoured, probably maliciously, that their seamanship suffered.[Note 2] The ship is said to have been 'in the bay in the afternoon' (i.e. the afternoon of February 10th, 1799) 'and as people went to church the seafaring men felt some anxiety if the wind should shift a point and blow as it afterwards did. They made every effort to get out to sea and kept firing signals of distress'. In the absence of any kind of lifeboat service in the late 18th century, no one could go to their rescue.

On the centenary of the wreck the curator of the North Devon Athenaeum in Barnstaple, Thomas Wainwright, brought out a leaflet giving an account of the disaster and the recovery and sale of salvaged goods. The ship, he said, 'while under sail, standing off to the westward, in a tempestuous gale of wind, became embayed as it were between Lundy Island and Baggy Point, and at one a.m. on the 11th struck on a rock, situated almost close to the shore, since known as the "Weazle rock," was dashed to pieces and all on board (the crew 105 and one woman) perished with her. One of the crew had been left on shore, and so escaped the fate of his companions'.

Only eighteen bodies were recovered intact and buried. The rest. Wainwright says, were picked up on the rocks at Croyde and Baggy Hole, 'without arms, legs or clothing to distinguish them, while about thirty years ago seven skeletons buried in the sand were uncovered by the high tide'.

Tradition gives the name of the woman as Nancy Golding. Like Wainwright, Georgeham's burial register oddly records her as part of the crew. The entry, which appears between others dated April 3rd and May 30th, 1799 – and thus nearly two months after the wreck – reads: 'The bodies of nine men and one woman, part of the crew of the *Weazle* sloop-of-war, lost in Barnstaple Bay on the 11th day of February, were buried on the south side of the churchyard'. The

tombstone of just one of them, William Kidman of Huntingdon, aged 23, is known, and survives, propped against the church tower. Six bodies – one of them that of Lieut. Butler – were found at Woolacombe and buried at Mortehoe. The surgeon, William Grey, was found at Saunton and buried at Braunton, although much of his property, including a medical chest and boxes of instruments, came in at Woolacombe.

Nancy Golding's presence aboard has never been explained. It is of course possible that she was smuggled aboard by one of the crew – even, possibly, in place of the seaman who was left on shore, though it is hardly likely that she was disguised in sailor's clothes, like one of the love-lorn girls who formed the surprising crew commanded by Lieut. Belaye in W.S. Gilbert's *The Bumboat Woman's Story*.

The crew list included a number of 'boys second class' and 'boys third class'. Many were local, from Appledore, Ilfracombe, Northam, Heanton and Torrington. One boy is said to have survived, but if so, there seems to be no record of what became of him. Also on the ship was Thomas Dunsford, a pilot from Appledore, yet it is evident that his presumably extensive knowledge of Barnstaple Bay and its weathers could not prevent the loss of the *Weazle* – unless it happened that Captain Grey overrode his advice.

Wainwright was able to quote from a contemporary 'account of the charges of Saving, preserving and disposing of the Wreck of His Majesty's sloop of war, *Weazle* lately stranded with the appurtinces thereunto belonging at the Southward of Baggy Point, in a place called and known by the name of Cride Sands in Barnstaple Bay, it being the Royalty of P. R. Webber, Esq., on the 11th day of February, 1799.'

The largest single charge was a Richard Budd's, 'for himself and horse, 15 days and 14 nights at 2s.6d per day and 2s.6d per night; £3.12s.6d'. Although it seems improbable that Richard Budd and his horse worked by night and well as day, the fact that it took over a fortnight to gather up all the wreckage is an indication of the large quantity recovered. On March 27th, Richard Budd acted as auctioneer at John Smith's house, and charged a guinea for his trouble, as well as a further 31s.6d for his work between February 26th and March 12th. John Smith himself appears in several entries; he hired out horses and carts, looked after the salvage and charged 16 shillings for 'washing and preserving of Hammicks and difft. Clothing'. (Among the clothing was a pair of trousers and a pair of pantaloons which had belonged to the purser, and were given to the seaman who had been left ashore.)

Twelve shillings were spent on ale 'for the carpenters and people working on the rocks at different times', and less than half that amount for ale for 'the men Saving the gun'. Total charges for the twenty or so men employed for odd days came to about thirty pounds. Just over a ton of copper sheets sold at ninepence a pound at the auction; iron bolts went for elevenpence three farthings; lead was twelve shillings a hundredweight. There were barrels and pipe staves, thirty fathoms of 'junk of cable', twenty four blankets and a Union Jack, as well as twenty-three hammocks which sold, in three lots, for nearly thirty shillings. The Revd Thomas Hole was rector of Georgeham at this time; he bought part of the foremast and three separate lots of 'wrack', paying six guineas in all. A Captain Horden spent £2.4s on a sail, a cot, some hammocks and one lot of 'wrack', a Captain Goldsberry bought the mainmast for six guineas and a Captain Cutcliffe contented himself with a 'Tarpolin' for 1s 2d and some 'wrack' for 2s 6d. These may have been retired naval officers, but it is more likely that they were the skippers of local coasting ketches or fishing boats, and had come from Braunton or Ilfracombe for the sale.

Wainwright said that the grandson and namesake of the John Smith 'who had charge of the property is now resident in the village (Croyde) and has afforded me valuable assistance in my enquiries'. This would have been the local character known as Muggy Smith, to whom Henry Williamson devoted a chapter in *Life in a Devon Village.*Note 3 He had been born at the Manor Inn, but as a young man sold the property and went to America, where he claimed to have led a wild life. He came back to Croyde in late middle age, and lived to be 75, eking out a frugal living by selling such things as rabbit skins and water cress, liking to talk to summer visitors and tell them jokes. He died suddenly in 1929.

Two years before the *Weazle* wreck there had been a seaborne drama of a different kind. Since 1793 England and France had been at war (which makes the fact that smuggled goods, mostly from France, could have been brought across the Channel, and caused a warship to be diverted to preventive work, somewhat surprising). These were, however, only the early stages of the long-drawn out series of conflicts that would not end until the defeat of Napoleon in 1815. A meeting of the magistrates of Devon was called by Earl Fortescue at Exeter in April, 1794. Proposals were put forward to form volunteer companies in a number of towns, especially near the coast, to augment existing militia; there were also to be troops of Fencible cavalry.[Note 4] Lieut. Col. Orchard, commanding the North Devon Volunteers, wrote from Hartland Abbey on 23rd February, 17987, to report to the Duke of Portland that he had received an 'express' from Ilfracombe saying that there were three French frigates off that place, that they had scuttled several merchantmen and were trying to destroy shipping in the harbour. He called out the volunteers and ordered them to be ready to march, but before they could set off a second message arrived saying that the French ships were gone from the coast and all was well. Col. Orchard evidently thought it prudent to take the whole thing with a pinch of salt. 'How far the report was well founded, I cannot possibly say, but, as the affair may be misrepresented and exaggerated, I trust your Grace will excuse my troubling you with this letter'. He was right to be sceptical; no merchantmen had been scuttled, and there had been no attack on Ilfracombe harbour. Philip Rogers Webber, mentioned as the owner of Croyde sands at the time of the *Weazle* wreck, noted in his diary that on February 22nd two French ships and a lugger had passed Lundy heading for Ilfracombe, the alarm being raised about midnight, though by break of day no vessel was to be seen.

Nevertheless, all sorts of rumours of imminent invasion must have been flying along the coast from Clovelly to Croyde, Mortehoe and Ilfracombe, and the people of Georgeham were probably as apprehensive as any. The parish was to have its own company of Volunteers, though not, it seems, until 1798. By the spring of 1799 it had a lieutenant and second lieutenant, three sergeants, three corporals, two drummers and 64 privates. Among them were men with surnames which would still be familiar in the village in the first half of the 20th century – Bagster, Clibbett, Ellis, Gammon, Lovering, Norman, Thomas and Tucker.

It seems possible that a number of men from Georgeham parish served in the army or navy during the Napoleonic wars, but only one can be identified. He was Sergeant John Hill of the 40th Regiment of Infantry. As his well-cared-for gravestone, conspicuously placed on the right of the path running from the lychgate to the south door of the

the church records, he was a 'Waterloo man'; he also served through the Peninsular War with Wellington's army. He was 77 when he died in 1862, so would have been 31 in the year of Waterloo. As no John Hill appears in the register of baptisms for 1784, his presumed year of birth, Georgeham does not seem to have been his native village. However, he lived out his days as an army pensioner at Netherham Cottage, on the right of the road leading out of Georgeham towards Putsborough. In White's Directory of Devon, published in 1850, his name appears between those of the Revd Francis Hole and W. Vellacott Richards, Esq., Incledon House, as 'Hill, John, Sergeant' as though he was regarded as one of the gentry. Certainly, during the long years of his retirement, he must have acquired a reputation as an outstanding local character.

6

Country Roads

adiating from Georgeham, like the web of an unpractised spider, run roads interconnected by lanes and tracks, all originally trodden out by the feet of men and horses. There are some six or seven ways of reaching Braunton and Saunton, and more than one of reaching Woolacombe and Mortehoe, though some may still only be followed on foot.

In earlier centuries, the roads of Devon were notoriously bad.'A county, as it is spacious, so it is populous, and the inhabitants very laborious, thorough, and unpleasant to Strangers travelling these Ways; which are cumbersome and uneven, among Rocks and Stones, painful for Man and Horse, as they can best witness who have made Tryal thereof, for be they never so well mounted on Horses out of other counties, when they have travelled one journey in these parts, they can, in respect of Ease of Travel, forbear a second'. That was the opinion of the Devon antiquarian writer, Tristram Risdon, writing in the first half of the 17th century, and the doughty traveller, Celia Fiennes, at the end of that century, was complaining that the lanes between Chudleigh and Ashburton were 'full of stones and dirt for the most part, because they are so close the sun and wind cannot come at them, so many places you travel on Causeys which are uneven for want of continual repair'.

In his poem, 'The Rolling English Road', G.K. Chesterton claimed that 'the rolling English drunkard made the rolling English road', but it might be more accurate to say that the hoofs of wandering packhorse trains, trying to avoid soft patches, made the tracks in country places that later became roads. On hills, the surface was often washed to the bare rock, with a central channel down which in rainy weather a quick stream flowed. The true lane of this century, lying six or eight feet below the level of surrounding fields, impassable to cars but rutted by tractors (or, until the late 1940s, the iron-bound wheels of farmcarts) is the good road of three centuries ago. Then, the poor road was so narrow that one loaded horse could not pass another. Travelling in strings, sure-footed on the stony or broken ground, packhorses carried woolpacks and bundles of woven cloth, peat, coal, corn, hay and straw, as well as the farm manures – lime, sand and dung. The walker or rider had to get out of their way as best he could: 'some little corners may jut out . . . but this but seldom,' remarked Celia Fiennes, and Charles Vancouver, writing a report on agriculture in Devon at the beginning of the 19th century, found that 'The rapidity with which these animals descend the hills, when not loaded, and the utter impossibility of passing loaded ones, require that the utmost caution should be used in keeping out of the way of the one, and exertion in keeping ahead of the other. A cross-way, fork in the road, or gateway, is eagerly looked for as a retiring spot to the traveller'.

As the number of horse-drawn vehicles increased, things became even worse – yet everyone knew that improvements would be costly. The answer seemed to be to charge for the use of roads. Tolls had been levied on bridges and certain roads from as early as the 14th century, and in 1555 parliament had passed the first of a long series of Acts which gradually ensured that local authorities became responsible for the upkeep of the highways. An Act of 1675 made it legal to erect turnpikes to exact tolls for the repair of part of the Great North Road, and from then on, despite considerable opposition and resentment, the turnpike principle began to be extended to many parts of the kingdom. It reached north Devon in 1763, when an Act was passed 'for repairing, widening and keeping in Repair several Roads leading from the town of Barnstaple'. Trustees were appointed to erect turnpikes in such places as they thought fit. Some exemptions from tolls could be claimed: for instance, carts carrying loads of various kinds (including, logically enough, road-building materials) and horses going to pasture, to water, or to be 'shoed or farried' were not charged.

The first Act expired after 21 years and was renewed in 1784. There were subsequent renewals in 1806, 1828, 1841 and finally in 1865. In 1879 the raising of road tolls in North Devon ended, and all turnpikes and toll houses were sold off.

None of the first six turnpike roads from Barnstaple led in the direction of Braunton or the villages to the north. However, in 1828, when trustees were empowered to make eight new roads, one was routed to Braunton via Ashford and Heanton Punchardon, and another from Braunton through Georgeham and Mortehoe to Ilfracombe. (One full toll was to be taken between Barnstaple and Braunton and two between Braunton and Ilfracombe.)[Note 1]

Many quarries must have been opened up to provide stone for all this road-building, adopting the method proposed by the Scotsman John Loudon McAdam: the use of thin layers of hard stone broken into 'angular fragments of a nearly cubical shape, and as nearly as possible of the same size, and no piece to weigh more than six ounces; the whole to be consolidated gradually by the passage of traffic over the road'.It is interesting that one of McAdam's grandsons, John Law, acted as clerk to the Barnstaple Turnpike Trust from 1806 to 1822, as Surveyor from 1822 to 1831, and as Treasurer from 1831 to 1845.

The trustees were men of local importance and influence, mostly landowners and gentry. No records seem to have survived of the names of those who officiated in 1763 and 1784, but in 1806 there were no fewer than 155 of them, including eleven members of the Chichester family and four of the Fortescue family. The clergy of many parishes evidently interested themselves in the Trust, so much so that nearly a third of all Trustees in 1827, 1841 and 1865 were parsons.For Georgeham, the Revd Thomas Hole and his son Francis were members in 1806, and the Revd Francis, having become rector in 1831, was a member in 1841 and 1865.

In 1841 tolls included a charge of sevenpence halfpenny 'For every horse or other beast drawing any coach, chariot, landau, chaise, chaise marine, car, calash, berlin, barouche, chair or other such light carriage', while 'For every horse or other beast drawing any stage coach, stage wagon, stage cart, caravan, omnibus or other such carriage, where more than one horse or beast is used' the toll was sixpence. Significantly, the appearance of a new type of vehicle was mentioned for the first time: 'For every carriage propelled or drawn by steam or other power than animal or manual power, sixpence'. It was just eleven years since the first regular railway service between Liverpool and Manchester had begun to run, making everyone aware of the potential of steam as motive power, and in 1830 the Exeter 'Flying Post' had reported that a public meeting had been held in Plymouth 'to consider the propriety of establishing a regular communication between the towns of Plymouth, Devonport and Stonehouse by means of a Steam Carriage . . . to which a barouche, stage coach or omnibus may be attached'.

John Ogilby's road map of 1675 shows a road from Ilfracombe via 'Stracom' (Spreacombe) to Georgeham which runs on to Saunton Court and across the Burrows to St. Anne's Chapel on the north shore of the Taw/Torridge estuary. This indicates that what is now a narrow unsurfaced lane over the hill behind South Hole Farm was then a main route for travellers making their way to a ferry crossing to Northam and Bideford and so, perhaps, into Cornwall. The map produced by the Bideford-born cartographer, Benjamin Donn, in 1765, offers a simplified version of this route, and a map of 1821 reveals that the road from Ilfracombe to Georgeham ran via Slade and Ossaborough and what is marked as Lower Spraycombe.[Note 2] On this map the old way from Saunton Court to what by this time had become merely the 'site' of St. Anne's Chapel is no more than a track.

The people of Georgeham must have become used to seeing packhorse trains making their way through the village in earlier centuries, but by the time the iron mines were opened at Spreacombe in the second half of the 19th century, the ore would have been carried away by horse and cart. The mines are said to have produced 118 tonnes of brown haematite in 1876, valued at £70. In all, only 779 tonnes were extracted; the venture was evidently not profitable, and ended in about 1890.[Note 3]

(Henry Williamson, exploring the Spreacombe valley during his holiday in May, 1914, saw 'a ruinous cottage, with a forge, washing trough, and other buildings'; it was 'a place of magpies, vipers and solitude'.)

The ore was taken to Velator Quay for shipment to Wales. It seems probable that the loads were not transported through Georgeham; more direct routes would have been either along Northfield Road and

down to Fairlinch Cross or through Spreacombe to what is now the main Ilfracombe-Braunton road, the A361. (Spreacombe valley has recently regained much of its ancient peacefulness after a second period of industrial disturbance: the extraction of roadstone from Vyse Quarry has come to an end.)

Chapel Wood, not far from the old mine workings, is now in the possession of the RSPB, and permission to visit it must be sought from the warden. The chapel which gave it its name was in existence by 1385, when the Bishop of Exeter granted a licence to William Cornu and Constance his wife for services to be held in the chapels of St. Martin and St. John the Baptist at Spreacombe. The first named may have been in William Cornu's house, but the second was almost certainly dedicated to John the Baptist because of the well nearby, which would have been venerated as a holy well, fed by a never-failing spring. It is thought to have fallen into disuse after the dissolution of all chantry chapels in 1562.

Permission to excavate the chapel was given in 1924 by Lady Arthur Cecil, who had bought Spreacombe Manor and about a hundred acres around it soon after the First World War. A building sixty feet by twenty was discovered; the chapel itself measured thirty-five feet by twenty, while the remainder may have been the priest's dwelling.[Note 4] In 1938 it was scheduled as an Ancient Monument.

The name Oxford Cross for the point where Mains Down Lane branches off to Spreacombe seems a misnomer. Henry Williamson insisted that some late-19th century surveyor misheard a local man who told him that it was Ox's Cross, and for that reason he gave the name to the field alongside the crossroads, and hence to the strangely designed house built for him during the last years of his life. Unfortunately the first Ordnance map of Devon, published in 1809, leaves the crossroads nameless. The area was once part of the Pickwell estate, and it is just possible that the name was the choice of the owner of Pickwell.

Some two hundred yards downhill from the crossroads, until the end of the 1920s, was a little quarry supplying a reddish roadstone. (It was filled in before the new cemetery was opened at that point.) No road in north-west Devon had been asphalted at that time. Quarried stone was transported in horse-drawn carts to roadside bays called standings, where stonecrackers worked, using knapping hammers to break the big lumps of stone to pieces small enough for road mending, and stacking them in neat heaps. These were measured by surveyors and paid for by the yard. Much of the stone in the neighbourhood of Georgeham was an iron-stained sandstone. Shoes and boots, the wheels of carts and of the few cars that passed were tinted with red mud in winter and pink dust in summer; potholes, filling with rainwater, became puddles the colour of weathered brick.

Henry Williamson sometimes talked to one of the stonemasons who frequented the Kings Arms, and found that he spoke 'good and simple English'; he wrote down some of his phrases, and later was astonished and delighted to discover the same phrases in Shakespeare. The man 'had not taken them from the book Shakespeare, but the living Shakespeare had taken them from common speech.Note 5

Some stonecrackers were former quarry workers who had lost an eye in an accident; they were supposed to wear protective goggles, but in my recollection did not do so. Stonecrackers must have been a familiar sight in most counties before roads were asphalted. Fred Weatherley, the prolific author of the words of hundreds of popular drawingroom ballads, including 'Thora', 'Nirvana' and 'Friend o' Mine', evidently saw them at work. His song, 'Stonecracker John' was set to music by the young Eric Coates, and published in 1909. A best-seller of the early years of the 20th century, *The Roadmender,* by Michael Fairless (Margaret Fairless Barber, 1869-1901) is written in the first person as though by a singularly well-educated and philosophical stonecracker.

The cracked stone was spread from carts by men with shovels and rakes, and rolled in by steamrollers each bearing on its front plate a gleaming brass figure of a prancing horse and the words 'Ruston Bucyrus', pronounced locally Ruston Buckyruss.

The earlier forerunner of the road linking the two valley villages of Georgeham and Croyde was probably a track used by Saxons; if so, they chose to follow the southern hillside for much of the way, skirting the tiny manor of North Hole and going on to ford the stream running down from Darracott. A short distance from the ford, across what may have been a marshy meadow, they would have seen it flow into the main valley stream. Even then a track probably turned off to branch at the manor of South Hole, one line going south over the hill and the other leading more directly to Braunton. Until the coast road from Saunton to Croyde was cut in 1907, anyone wanting to travel from Croyde to Braunton might have taken this road from Forda – or as it is marked on late 19th century maps, Ford. It was known locally in the first half of the 20th century as Old Cleave, but today's Ordnance Surveyors have it down as Hole Cleave. It rises to meet the road from Georgeham via Darracott. In the mid 1930s fields near the eastern end of Old Cleave were given over to bulb-growing, mostly daffodils and hyacinths, while down on the sandy levels behind Saunton Burrows were tulip fields, great blazing rectangles of red, pink, yellow and purple in May. The bulb farm was first established in the mid-1920s by Richard Cobley on one ten-acre field. Within a few years it had become a holding of 120 acres employing 140 people. All cultivation was by hand except the ploughing-out of the bulbs – which were then gathered by hand. The farm continued to operate until the 1960s; its last glasshouses were demolished by a gale in January, 1990.

The 1851 census shows a Thomas Holcote as the occupier of Hole Mill, below Forda. That mill evidently ceased to operate well before the end of the century. Beyond were what the census refers to as the 'villages' of Rumpet and Cross. A short lane, Veal Lane, runs up the hillside on the Georgeham side of Cross, to end in fields. Another, Pathdown Lane, runs up to join a track, once a lane; turning left, one may follow the ridge eastwards; turning right, it is possible to come down Mill Lane, which emerges opposite the site of Croyde Mill.

If that mill had still existed at the time of the flood of June, 1931, it might well have been severely damaged, but it had gone a few years earlier. Henry Williamson described seeing it working at some time in the mid-1920s. In a chapter called 'Village Inns' in *Life in a Devon Village* he referred to it as a Jacobean water mill, but in another he gave an account of being shown over the 'ancient grist mill at the head of Croyde village' and spoke of its Charles II millhouse. The miller told him it had belonged to his great-great-grandfather; he could just make it pay, but within a short time motor transport, bringing cheap factory-ground flour to the village, meant that he had to give it up. The millpond beside the road below Fig Tree Farm remained for a few years after the mill, with its great wheel transferring power to the grinding stones by a system of rumbling cogs, had been demolished and replaced by a dwelling.

At the side of the Manor Inn, the entrance to Combas Lane has become half-hidden since the development of Kittiwell as a hotel. Beyond Combas Farm it changes its name to Meadow Lane, and emerges beside the pond opposite one of the most beautiful old houses in the parish, Putsborough Manor, with its farmhouse behind it and its little stream that flows from the hillside to the north and make a watersplash across the road.

Little motorised traffic passed up and down the valley road in the 1920s. Children from Croyde could dawdle up to Georgeham school in the mornings, and dawdle home again in the afternoon, picking wild flowers as they went in spring and summer, in complete safety. Even though a regular bus service from Barnstaple to Georgeham began to run around the middle of the decade, after one or two earlier undertakings had failed, it would not have occurred to anyone that healthy children could not walk a couple of miles or so to and from school.

Horse-drawn vehicles still predominated. Farm carts carrying hay, potatoes, swedes or timber rumbled up or down on iron-rimmed wheels, each drawn by a single heavy horse, the carter plodding at its head. A carrier usually referred to as the oil man regularly visited the villages and farms; his stock-in-trade was the paraffin that every household in the district needed until electricity arrived in the late 1930s. His horse-drawn van, like a small covered wagon, was hung with brushes, brooms, mops, saucepans and clothes pegs, and stocked with candles, lamps, spare glass chimneys and wicks, crockery and assorted items ordered by housewives. A small, white, smooth-haired terrier bitch rode on the front seat. Her master claimed that she was a great age. She was always with him, sitting upright and watching the road; she had lost neither sight nor hearing.

Until the road from Saunton was cut, there was only a narrow bridge at the seaward end of Croyde. The stream flowed freely; no wall divided it from the road. Ducks swam in it; children played in it; people dipped water for washing from it; horses drank from it. On winter's nights, men emerging from the Carpenter's Arms or the Manor Inn occasionally fell into it. There were stepping stones at intervals to the houses on the further bank; later one or two small wooden bridges were built. The village had its own forge, and its own baker. It was, like most villages in the early years of the 20th century, more or less self-sufficient.

The last traces of the old way of life seems to have gone with the demolition of the mill. Soon afterwards came the asphalting of the road, and a wall was built along the stream. Croyde became more and more popular, not just as a place to visit, but as a place to live in. Housebuilding along the roads on either side of the bay began a process that after the Second World War would accelerate until a large suburban fringe lay between the village and the sea.

7

New Arrivals

hen Britain's first national census was taken in 1801, the population of Georgeham was 627. During the next fifty years the registers show that the number of baptisms exceeded the number of burials by anything from three to 27, the average being 25; in several years there were more than 30 births. As a result, by the time of the 1851 census the population had risen to 971. This surge in numbers followed a general national trend: between 1801 and 1901, the number of people in the United Kingdom trebled, rising from about eleven million to 33 million. A contributory factor was the provisions of the outdated Poor Law, originally passed in the last year of the life of Elizabeth I, 1601. According to a writer responding to a questionnaire sent out in 1816, the year after the Napoleonic War finally ended, to 'the most opulent and intelligent landowners in England, Wales and Scotland, the Poor Laws however humanely intended have been found from experience, to act as an encouragement to idleness and vice, and to promote those improvident marriages by which a population larger than the country can employ in the works of industry, is produced'. The system encouraged the lowest paid workers to have large families, as they could obtain outdoor relief paid out of the rates in proportion to the size of their families. Farmers therefore paid very low wages and very high rates, knowing their workmen would be compensated.

With the ending of the war, farmers found a sudden drop in the value of their produce. Many gave up their tenancies, and a good deal of land went out of cultivation. Even some seamen were affected; because less lime was being used to fertilise the fields, the little ships that had carried culm and stone from Wales for the coastal limekilns were laid up.[Note 1]

During the war, the rise in food prices had caused bread riots in a number of places. At best, the food of country people was very plain and monotonous; wheat or barley bread, potatoes provided by their employers, or grown on a plot of ground rented from them; once a year, possibly, a supply of pork or bacon, if the piece of ground was big enough to allow them to keep a pig. By the late 1820s, however, corn had become so dear that unrest spread westwards across the southern counties to reach the Barnstaple-South Molton area by the end of 1830. Disturbances were soon put down by the use of the local militia. There seems to be no record of farm workers in Georgeham and its immediate neighbourhood indulging in angry protest, but they can hardly have avoided experiencing the general level of acute poverty.

The sharp rise in numbers evidently produced some overcrowding, though this was perhaps nothing new. Whereas in 1801, 149 families were living in 141 house (there were 297 males and 330 females), in 1831 186 families were living in 176 houses (with six uninhabited and two being built.) Twenty years later the number of houses had increased to 204, yet for some reason the situation was little better than it had been half a century earlier: 188 families were living in 177 houses, while 17 were uninhabited. By that time the population was dropping to a level only a little above that in 1801, almost certainly because many members of large families had been forced to move elsewhere to find work. (All over Victorian England, country people migrated to the fast-growing industrial cities looking for jobs.) The 1891 census shows a remarkable total of 29 uninhabited houses, suggesting a considerable exodus.

By the 1830s it was realized that the medieval system of paying tithes, greatly resented, was no longer appropriate; the Tithes Commutation Act of 1936 provided for a monetary settlement, and Commissioners were appointed to negotiate land values in parishes. In 1839 Georgeham tithes were commuted for £500 a year. The Tithe

48

Apportionment schedule for the parish shows that some 2,700 acres – well over half its total area – were in the possession of six landowners. The largest estate was Pickwell, with 875 acres, which Earl Fortescue had bought in 1832. Charles Henry Webber owned 717 acres at Croyde, and the Revd Francis Hole owned 255. Most farms seem to have been small, and many properties were in effect smallholdings: 42 of them extended to no more than from one to twenty acres, while another seventeen ranged from twenty to fifty acres. One woman, Mary Ann Salteen, owned a 94-acres farm, but it was worked by a tenant; four other women had little plots of less than an acre. In the 1851 census, nineteen householders are women; most would presumably have been widows, though one or two may have been spinsters who had inherited property from their fathers.

Not surprisingly, the most common occupation was farm labourer, with farmer coming second. Villages were still largely self-sufficient, to an extent that seems remarkable today. William White's 1850 *Directory of Devon* lists four blacksmiths in Georgeham and two in Croyde; five boot and shoe makers in Georgeham and two in Croyde. There were still two corn millers in the parish, and several pubs of one sort or another. The Kings Arms was owned by Joseph Thomas and Rock House by Charles Conibear, who doubled as a blacksmith; both he and Thomas are described as victuallers. A William Lang, of Victoria House (now Millie's) is shown as a beerhouse keeper, though in Morris's *Commercial Directory* of 1870 he appears as a shoemaker, farmer and beer retailer. Robert Scamp was a maltster and victualler at the Ring o' Bells, at what would later become West End Farm. (The surname Scamp occurs frequently in the parish registers: as early as 1540 a Thomas, son of John Scamp, was baptised. It is possible that a Robert Scamp who married Sally Brace in 1821 was the maltster.)

The fashion for seaside holidays had its origin in the mid-18th century, when a Dr Russell, from Lewes, put forward the theory that sea-bathing and even *drinking* seawater was a remedy for all kinds of ailments. He chose Brighton, then a small village, as a suitable base from which to spreads his ideas. Invalids who could afford it were soon trying the new cure, and before long even those who were not ill began to discover the attractions of the coast. When the Prince Regent and his entourage arrived in Brighton in 1783, the place developed rapidly. Yet even before then, other places found themselves

welcoming visitors; it is slightly surprising to learn that as early as 1771 the Exeter 'Flying Post', referring to Ilfracombe, announced:

'Arrived here, for the benefit of the Air, Salt Water and to spend part of the Summer Season, Miss McDonald, Mrs Pynes, Mrs Knot, Mrs Hill, Mrs Spurway and Mrs Servant; Captain Fraine and Family will be here Tomorrow; Captain Vallarot, who spent some time here, intends to set off for Gibraltar, where his Regiment now is. Of the very many persons who had frequented Ilfracombe for their health, during the Summer season, for Years past, but one have (sic) died, so salubrious is its Air and Waters'.

By 1788 the 'Flying Post' was reporting Ilfracombe 'remarkably full of genteel company, being resorted to by members of very respectable families from most parts of the country. What pleases strangers most is the conveniency of the bathing machines, and the great attention of the townspeople to accommodate them'. Three years later the *Universal British Directory* was describing the town as 'pleasant and convenient place for bathing and much resorted to by the gentry for that purpose'.

The existence of bathing machines and accommodation acceptable to the gentry and 'genteel company' in late 18th century Ilfracombe is the more unexpected when it is considered that travelling to north Devon cannot have been easy. The road improvements that were to follow the introduction of turnpike roads had not yet begun; passengers in coaches or private carriages must have jolted uncomfortably along roads that by today's standards were no more that country lanes, even if in summer they were dusty rather than deep in mud. Journeys were inevitably slow; in 1871 Fanny Burney, the diarist and immensely popular novelist of her day, took twenty-four hours to travel by coach from Bath to Barnstaple, without pausing for the night, by way of Bristol, Bridgewater, Taunton and South Molton. Yet the 'Flying Post' made it clear that once a seaside town had gained a name as a place in which to spend the summer season, whether for health or simply pleasure, people were willing to undergo the tedium of travelling to reach it.

It is just possible that some of Ilfracombe's visitors in the late 18th or early 19th centuries hired horses or carriages to make a cautious way westwards, and found themselves in Georgeham or Croyde, but when Pigot and Co's *National Commercial Directory* appeared in 1830, the two villages were evidently not considered important enough to be noticed. It was another twenty years before a country directory included an entry which began:

'Georgeham, a small straggling village, in a valley 8 miles W.S.W. of Barnstaple, has in its parish 923 souls and 4050 acres of land, extending westwards to Croyde and Morte Bays, and the long narrow promontory called Baggy Point, where the rocky cliffs rise boldly from the Bristol Channel. Most of the parishioners are in the villages and hamlets of Croyde, North Buckland, Darracott and Putsborough. Croyde is a pleasant sea bathing place, with a fine bay, and much romantic scenery in its vicinity'.Note 2

By 1870, there is a mention of 'good lodging houses for the accommodation of visitors', and nineteen years later John Gammon, at Moorpark House, was offering lodgings, William Reed, a farmer, ran a lodging house with two sitting rooms and eight bedrooms; he also had horses and carriages for hire. The Manor Inn was called The Manor House Hotel. Most impressive of all was James Holwill's lodging house in Somerset Place: its situation, facing the sea, was described as charming; it had fourteen bedrooms and six sitting rooms.

By that time the railway had entirely changed the speed and ease of travel. Although it did not reach Ilfracombe until 1874, Barnstaple had given a rapturous welcome to its first train twenty years earlier. In the interval, visitors could complete their journeys by coach. Coach roads had improved considerably since the first half of the century, and not everyone enjoyed train travel. George Eliot, the novelist, having arrived at Barnstaple by train from London, via Exeter, in 1853, seems to have greatly preferred what she called 'the good old stagecoach' in which she completed her journey to Ilfracombe.

Yet although by the late 1870s the railway had made Braunton, Croyde and Mortehoe more accessible than they had ever been, Georgeham, lying inland, may as yet have seen few visitors, except those who decided to explore on foot or horseback from their lodgings in Croyde, so it seems possible that life in the village was much as it had been a hundred years earlier.

8

Changes in the Church.

A brief description of Georgeham church as it was in the 18th century was provided by Benjamin Incledon, a keen antiquarian who was Recorder of Barnstaple from 1758 to 1796. He made his visit in 1771. The Revd William Chichester died the previous year; his successor, John Sanford, was living 'in a parsonage house presented by Sir John Chichester of Youlston', which indicates that Sir John, as patron of the living, had not only appointed his younger brother to it, but had built a new rectory for him. He had also had some work done on the interior of the church. Mr Incledon (whose spelling and grammar are his own) noted that 'Over the Gallery is wrote "This church was beautified in 1762. Richard But(ler?), James Butler, Wardens". The church is very handsomely decorated – it consists of two Isles with seats or rather pews of wainscot oak panelled, circular head sash windows, a very rich stucco ceiling and Cornish Cornice?) with the king's arms equally well executed – the Gallery of the same material as the seats. Under the Great Arch between the chancel and the Harris aisle lies the Effigies of a man in full proportion and armour, crossed legs, two angels support his head and two Lions are at his feet. I think this may be Mauger St. Aubyn'.[Note 1]

John Davidson, who saw the church in 1832, observed that it was an

53

ancient church modernised throughout, 'the windows Romanised except one in the chancel'. The gallery, which reached across the nave and south aisle, bore the coats of arms of Chichester, Newcourt, Harris, Dinham and Gwyn.[Note 2]

An indefatigable Victorian investigator of churches (he is said to have visited 5,530 in all) was Sir Stephen Glynne.[Note 3] In 1860 he was not impressed by the interior of the church. 'Several windows have been modernised and the Chancel much disfigured by frippery modern work. The roofs are covered with ribs and bosses. In the porch as well as elsewhere . . . Tower arch and Chancel both modernised, the latter with stucco, which has been largely employed in ornamentation of the chancel and its S. Aisle, in mixed Gothic and Italian forms. Dividing the S. Chancel is a wood screen and the arch has been quite metamorphosed'.[Note 4]

These first-hand accounts all have a special interest in that they show the church as it was before it underwent a radical rebuilding in 1876 at a reported cost of about £3,500, mostly given by the then patron of the living, Thomas Hole, and his family. An almost contemporary report provides a detailed description of the work carried out:

'A church appears to have existed here as early as the 12th century, and to have extended further to the north than the present building, or the one which it replaced. Evidences of a doorway were found on pulling down the north wall, and during the necessary excavations outside the church on this side, portions of an ancient tiled floor were also discovered; these were carefully preserved and are in the possession of the Rev. W.C. Morcom. The church now consists of chancel and nave, the latter being separated from the south aisle and Pickwell chapel by an arcade of five arches; and at the west end is a lofty tower containing six bells, which have been recently re-hung. The roof of the nave is of English oak relieved with bosses, some of which are restored from the former church; and the new ones are exact copies of the old. The seats of the nave and aisle are open and of pitch pine; and the floor is paved with Minton's tiles, as is that of the chancel; but the tiles of the latter are of a more elaborate pattern. The handsome carved Caen stone pulpit, which with appropriate book-rests is the gift of Mrs. Crawshay, stands at the north-east corner of the nave, and has beautiful alabaster panels, on which are carved John the Baptist preaching in the wilderness, The Sermon on the Mount, and Paul at Athens. On the north side of the pulpit is the entrance to the ancient rood-loft, which was discovered while pulling down the north wall and has been preserved. The lectern and the chancel fittings are of oak. The reredos is a bas-relief of the Last Supper, and has been beautifully carved in stone by Messrs Ruddock and Sons, of London; at the side are four tablets of Caen stone with pillars of Devonshire marble. The East window is filled with stained glass, designed by Messrs. Lavers, Barraud and Westlake, in memory of the Rev. Francis Hole, rector of this parish, who died October 4, 1866, and was erected by his widow. In the south wall of the chancel is a window depicting the Good Samaritan, in remembrance of Captain Geo. Chichester (died March 20, 1872) by whose widow it was inserted, and in the north wall is a small quatrefoil window, found in the wall of the old church, and which has been filled with stained glass by Mr. D. Bell, at the expense of the rector. On removing the north wall, there was also found the remains of a stone carving, representing a Calvary group, which had, in all probability, at one time formed a portion of an altar piece: it was preserved as it was discovered, and now forms the back of a credence table. A piscina was found in the south wall of the chancel, and another in the Pickwell chapel. This chapel belongs to the Fortescue family, and has been restored at their expense. In a recess in the south wall is the recumbent figure of a Crusader, carved in stone, and supposed to be a memorial of Sir Mauger St. Aubyn; and here are also monuments to the Harris, Hole and other families. The font, which stands beneath the tower, is of stone handsomely carved. The west window, four lights, is filled with rich stained glass, executed by Mr. D. Bell, in memory of the Rev. Francis Hole, the late rector, who died Aug. 10, 1871, and was erected by his widow, Mary Brooking Hole, who died May 9, 1874'.[Note 5] (The second Francis Hole, born in 1824, was a son of the Revd Francis who died in 1866).

This report notes that 'Simon Gould and his wife Juliana, who died in March, 1817, each in the 101st year of their age, and having been married upwards of 75 years' were buried in the churchyard. (Later centenarians were Robert Fox, who died on 15th October, 1823, aged 104, and Elizabeth Boyles, who died on 28th January, 1829, aged 101).

There were three other places of worship in the parish: the small church of St. Mary Magdalene in Croyde, built in 1874 at a cost of £500, the Baptist chapel, built in 1816 and rebuilt in 1838 at a cost of

£100, with accommodation for 200 people, and the Wesleyan chapel in Georgeham, built in 1824, which could seat 90.

St. Mary Magdalene's had a school within the building. It was used as an infant school, and had an average attendance of 25 in 1883, when the mistress was a Miss Mary Ann Harris. By that time older children had to walk the two miles to school in Georgehem. The little schools first established as the result of John Richards' bequest, augmented by the Revd Thomas Hole, must have become inadequate for the increasing number of children in the parish by the mid-19th century. However, a directory of 1856 shows that there was still a schoolmistress in each village: Mrs Elizabeth Butler in Croyde and Miss Betty Davis in Georgeham. No school buildings seem to have existed then: each woman would have used a single cottage room. By 1866 there were said to be 'schools for boys and girls, partly endowed; John Bale, master'. The endowment came largely from a bequest of £400 left by William Vellacott: half the interest was to be distributed to the poor, and the other half 'applied to the education of poor children'. (The churchwardens' accounts for 1858 show that 'School-money' was payable twice a year, and amounted to £5.16s.3d, while another £5.17s.3d from Mr Vellacott's gift to 'Labourers, Paupers and Mechanics' was given out on the Sunday before Christmas Day.) All the varied bequests had come under the control of the Charity Commissioners by 1867.

At last, in 1868, the school building at the west end of Georgeham, still in use, was constructed, though it does not seem to have been opened until the following year, or to have accepted pupils until 1874, unless the first attendance register was lost.

In some parishes, churchwardens' accounts are in existence dating back as far as the 17th century, and are of considerable interest for the glimpse of social history they contain. Unfortunately, those for Georgeham survive only from 1855, when George Smith and Richard Howard recorded 'what they have received and expended from Easter 1854 to Easter 1855'. At that time the church rate (levied on all freehold and leasehold properties until 1868) was a penny in the pound; the total for the year was £13.16.7 1/4d, which would represent a total property value of just over £3,000. The clerk's salary was three pounds a year, the sexton's £1.12s.10d, and the 'chimers' – bellringers, presumably – were paid a guinea. In 1856 six shillings was spent on washing surplices, eightpence on a pound of candles,

sixpence on bread for the sacrament and three and sixpence on a bushel of coals. Four years later the sexton was paid thirteen shillings for 'cleaning the Church and walks etc.'; Joseph Thomas received five and tenpence for 'repairing seats, etc.' and Richard Pearce was paid twelve shillings and eleven pence for 'repairing, Healing and White Liming the Church' (Mary Ann Thomas received tenpence for 'Carriage of Lime'.) The church was repainted at a cost of six pounds ten shillings. This of course was the old building before the 'restoration' of 1876. 'Healing' meant tiling, so evidently the roof needed attention at this time. In 1865 slates, nails and timber were bought to repair its north side.

The actual restoration work evidently began in 1875, as in that year Eliza Brown was paid one pound ten shillings for cleaning and arranging the School Room for services; she continued to do this until October of the following year.

Two tons seven hundredweight of coke, presumably for heating the newly rebuilt church, cost one pound five shillings in 1876; carriage via the turnpike (which one was not specified) added another sixteen shillings. It looks as though oil lamps were introduced in the 1880s, as casks of petroleum were bought from time to time; in 1890, 42 gallons of oil cost one pound eight shillings.

A new organ was installed in 1881 as a memorial to Frances Hole, the wife of the rector who died in 1866, and a Mr Vowle began to receive a yearly payment for 'regulating' the instrument. An organ blower had to be employed; in 1913 he was receiving ten shillings as his half-yearly salary.

It seems unlikely that many men from Georgeham joined the army during the Boer War, but in 1914 the general urge to take part in what was referred to from the outset as the Great War persuaded a number of villagers to volunteer – and possibly some were conscripted.

During the war church collections were sometimes donated to such organizations as the Prince of Wales' War Fund, the Devon Patriotic War Fund, the Red Cross and Lord Kitchener's Memorial Fund. In 1915 the Belgian Refugees' Fund received a modest twelve shillings and sixpence. Later there were donations to the Prisoners of War Fund and the Blind Soldiers' Fund and – during the Twenties – to St. Dunstan's.

In memory of those who died on active service a new clock was installed in the church tower in June, 1921, at a cost of £230, subscribed in the parish, and the Bishop of Exeter dedicated a brass tablet in the church at what the 'North Devon Journal' described as an impressive service very largely attended. The inscription reads: 'To the glory of God and in honoured memory of the following members of the parish who laid down their lives in the Great War 1914-19. Killed in action: Andrews, W., 2nd Devons; Lang, P.F., 2nd Devons; Lovering, W.H., 17th Worcs; Incledon, A.W., R.A.M.C. Died on service: Lang, W.J., R. Navy; Tucker, F., R.M. Art.; White, C.G., Mon. Reg$^{t.}$ "Their name liveth for evermore".

The villages to which the survivors returned had probably changed hardly at all since 1914. In fact, as in many small villages of the time – especially in a county as remote from London as Devon – it was in some ways as though the Victorian age had hardly ended. Croyde, because it attracted a slowly increasing number of holiday makers, may have seemed less isolated, but Georgeham remained almost untouched by outside influences. There were no mains services in either village. Water was pumped from wells, stored in large butts or dipped from the valley stream; cottages were heated by coal or wood fires; cooking was on coal-fired ranges known as bodleys, or on oil stoves (a few villagers still used the cloam – clay-lined – wall ovens); oil lamps and candles were lit after dark. The only street lighting came dimly through curtained windows. Household rubbish was burned or buried in gardens. Very occasionally a car or lorry passed on the rough, stonemetalled roads, but the more familiar vehicles were horse-drawn carts, pony traps or the carrier's van. On farms in the area, tractors were unknown; all farm machinery except the steam threshing machines that visited in autumn were horse-drawn.

Yet changes were to come more and more rapidly during the inter-war years. For the twenties, an evocative though highly individual record survives in the writing of a man who lived in Georgeham for just eight years of the decade.

9

Henry Williamson's Georgeham

I n May, 1914, a youth of eighteen arrived at Braunton by train from London. (The journey at that time took about 5½ hours.) He was met by a horse and trap and driven to Georgeham, where he had arranged to stay for a fortnight with the postmistress, a Miss Watts. He had never visited the village before; it seems that he chose it on the recommendation of an aunt, a schoolmistress who had apparently enjoyed a holiday in Devon herself.

He spent the days walking, exploring tirelessly, enraptured by this new countryside. Those two weeks were the beginning of an association with Georgeham that would last, despite long absences, for the rest of his life. His name was Henry Williamson.

He was born in Brockley, in the London borough of Lewisham, on December 1st, 1895, but for a long time he pretended to be a year younger than he was, to accord with a fantasy of having joined the army straight from school at the age of seventeen. In fact he was eighteen when he left school at the end of the summer term of 1913. His father, who worked for the Sun Insurance Company, found him a job in a branch of the firm. Soon after starting work, Henry joined the Territorials: the four pounds paid to recruits in peacetime was a welcome bonus to a boy earning a clerk's wage in 1913. As a result he had no need to volunteer when war broke out: members of the Territorial Army were called up at once. He went to France with the 5th Battalion of the London Rifle Brigade in November, 1914, witnessed the remarkable Christmas Truce on the Western Front soon after his nineteenth birthday, and was invalided home early in 1915 with dysentery and trench feet (the latter not the military crime it became later). Having recovered, he obtained a commission, being gazetted as a second lieutenant in April, 1915. On July 1st, 1916, the first day of the appalling battle of the Somme, he was wounded. It was a wound that may well have saved his life, ensuring that he was taken to hospital in England again and that he had no further part in the continuing fighting of that terrible summer. Granted sick leave, he made for Georgeham again and, now much changed, renewed himself in its remote peace.

He later attended a course for transport officers at Belton Park, Grantham, and served with 208 Company, Machine Gun Corps, as a transport officer, at the time of Third Ypres (Passchendaele). In the last year of the war he was on home service, acting as adjutant – though as he himself recorded, in a very desultory way – at a Rest Camp in Folkestone. Coming upon a copy of Richard Jefferies' *The Story of my Heart* in a secondhand bookshop, he was momentarily transfixed; he stood in the shop reading the book for an hour before buying it. Its effect on him was profound. He had already made some attempt at writing novels and a number of wildlife sketches. Now he was confirmed in his determination to make writing the purpose of his life.

His army career ended at Brocton Camp, Staffordshire, in the autumn of 1919. Once again he made for Georgeham, and spent a short time there with a young married woman with whom he had fallen in love at Folkestone; she appears in his novels as Evelyn Fairfax. She seems to have had a number of lovers, and soon left Henry for someone else, to his dismay. He went back to his parents' home in Brockley. His grandfather found him a job in Fleet Street selling advertising space, and for a few months he wrote a column on what were then called 'Light Cars' for the *Weekly Despatch*. This came to an end in January, 1921, when the editor decided that Henry's contributions were becoming too facetious. At about the same time mutual recriminations between Henry and his father, whose disposition and outlook on life were totally dissimilar, came to a head.

Ordered to leave, he rode westwards on his beloved Norton motorcycle. In 1919 he had rented a cottage in Georgeham at about a shilling a week, and sublet it when his affair with 'Evelyn Fairfax' ended. Now it was presumably untenanted. He had somewhere to live, and something to live on: his first novel, *The Beautiful Years,* had been accepted for publication by Collins, he had a small disability pension, and he was confident that he could go on making money by writing.

The cottage he rented was one of three – formerly four – alongside the stream that flowed down beside the church wall. Built of cob, and thatched, it had two lime-washed bedrooms, a single living room with a kitchen range, and no other amenities at all. After the terrors and hardships of trench warfare in France he was indifferent to the conventional comforts of the life he had known before the war; the cottage suited him perfectly. ·

A photograph taken in the summer of 1921 shows him standing outside the white door of his cottage, on which he had written 'Skirr Cottage' in letters several inches high. Below this he had painted a version of the owl symbol which was to appear on his books.

For a few months he shared the cottage with the friend he refers to in several of his books as Julian Warbeck: a young ex-RAF officer whose capacity for beer – without, it seems, suffering any ill effects – was phenomenal. After a time there was a falling out, and 'Julian' went back to London. Henry continued work on his second novel, his only companions a spaniel puppy, a small cat, and various injured birds he had found, or which had been brought to him by villagers. By day, he walked for miles, as in May, 1914; in the evenings he visited the Rock Inn or the Kings Arms and listened to the talk that provided him with material for articles on country life that he could sell to newspapers. In 1922 the first of his collections of nature essays, *The Lone Swallows,* was published; the second, *The Peregrine's Saga,* came out the following year. By 1924 he was the author of five published books, his novels *Dandelion Days* and *The Dream of Fair Women* having followed *The Beautiful Years.* In that year he met his future wife, Ida Loetitia Hibbert. They were married in May, 1925.

By the end of the summer Loetitia knew that she was pregnant, and Henry at last acknowledged that it was time to find somewhere less primitive to live. Barely fifty yards from Skirr Cottage was Vale House. In the 1839 Tithe Apportionment it appears as Crowberry

Cottage, and a later owner reverted to the old name. In 1906 a Captain Venner Davidson was living there, and it is possibly he who renovated what may have been a simple cottage, adding a kitchen at the back and an outbuilding, later used as a garage, at one side; he may also have changed the name, though this is only conjecture. In about 1920 my grandmother bought the house, and let it. She lived in Barnstaple; my grandfather was vicar of St Mary Magdalene, a church which no longer exists. In 1925 her tenants, two elderly spinsters, had died within a few months of one another; the house stood empty. It was arranged that Henry and Loetitia should move in.

During his years in Skirr Cottage Henry had for a short time had an otter cub as a pet. Somehow, running in the fields, it trod on one of the cruel gin traps, set for rabbits, which were then legal. When he released it, it ran away, and he never saw it again, although he searched for it often. He wrote a number of stories about otters, and planned a book to be called *The Otter's Saga.* (It was while seeking accurate information about otter hunting that he met Loetitia at a meet of the Cheriton Otter Hounds on the Torridge; her father, Charles Hibbert, was one of the oldest members.) However, he set the early drafts aside while he finished *The Dream of Fair Women,* and only returned to what was to become *Tarka the Otter* after his marriage. He took over as his writing place a room above the garage beside the house. It was – and is – a light room with windows on two sides, a door into the raised garden and another, with glass panels, leading by way of a tiny balcony to one of the bedrooms. When it rained, the drops drummed noisily on the corrugated iron roof and, lacking any form of heating, must have been cold in winter but, for Henry, creature comforts never seem to have been of much importance.

For some reason he liked to give the impression that he lived at Skirr Cottage throughout his first eight years in Georgeham. To those who did not know the village he would often address his letters from there, safe in the knowledge that the postman would deliver any answers correctly. In his published writings, Vale House is not named. In consequence, some of those who visit the village to gaze at the cottage ignore the small house nearby, with its garden seven or eight feet above the level of the street. His reasons can only be guessed at. Skirr, with its romantic sounding name recalling the title of Blackmore's *The Maid of Sker,* had been his first home in Devon. The four years he had spent there, writing in a sort of frenzy of creativity, were a halcyon time he was to look back to with nostalgia for the rest of his life. Vale House, by contrast, saw the beginning of family cares and dissatisfactions – and its name may have sounded to him prim and suburban.

Yet it was at Vale House that he had written all the later drafts of *Tarka,* and finally completed the book. Its publication in 1927 had been followed by the award of the Hawthornden Prize for Literature, which established his name as an author. It was at Vale House that he had written *The Pathway,* the final volume of the tetralogy he called *The Flax of Dream* and the first of his non-animal novels to sell in large numbers. There too he had written his account of a journey to visit battlefields of the First World War, *The Wet Flanders Plain,* and a short novel about a private soldier's experiences in the war, *The Patriot's Progress,* as well as essays and nature stories making up *The Old Stag* and *The Linhay on the Downs,* and the sketches of life in Georgeham which appeared originally as *The Village Book* and *The Labouring Life* (later revised and republished as *Tales of a Devon Village* and *Life in a Devon Village*). It was at Vale House that he was visited, to his delight, by his hero T. E. Lawrence in July, 1929. Finally it was while he and Loetitia lived in that house that their first two sons were born.

By the later 1920s he had grown weary of life in Georgeham. It had been an invaluable source of material to him, but as he was to write many years later, in *A Clear Water Stream,* he had wanted to escape from the noise of the village, 'about which I had written all I knew in two books, and as the place was beginning to "open up" as the local councillors said – red iron-stone dust of the roads making the limewashed cottage walls pink from passing motor cars – it had seemed good to depart'.

Perhaps another reason for going was that the attitude of the villagers to him was changing also. Once he had been a sort of local jester, and enjoyable subject of gossip and laughter, an oddity; as he himself expressed it, 'an author of sorts who was always talking about fame and success and yet remained steadily unfamous and unsuccessful'. Now a measure of success and fame had arrived and some of his less worldly-wise neighbours resented it – especially as they exaggerated the amount of money his books were bringing him.

One final act of absurdity had caused scandal and annoyance; at Whitsun, 1929, together with his friend John Heygate and another companion, he had glued newspaper over the new village sign, painted by Margaret Kemp-Welch, which had been set up outside the village hall. A letter of apology published in the *North Devon Journal* in August (dated, characteristically, from Skirr Cottage, and not Vale House) had, if anything, made things worse by introducing a rambling and not very convincing reason for his action.

Henry already knew Castle Hill, Filleigh, the family seat of the Fortescue family for many hundred years. One day he heard that a cottage there was to let. The estate was at this time the property of the fourth Earl Fortescue, one of whose brothers, Sir John, had written an introduction to *Tarka the Otter* which had almost certainly helped the sales of the book. (At the time he wrote it, he was approaching the end of his great thirteen-volume *History of the British Army*, begun in 1899.) After visiting Filleigh to look at the cottage, Shallowford, Henry and Loetitia went to the agent's office and declared themselves eager to take the cottage and the two miles of trout fishing that went with it. At Michaelmas, 1929, Henry became its new tenant.

At Shallowford, as at Georgeham, he would spend eight years. Leaving there in 1937, he would farm in Norfolk for yet another eight-year period, until finally he would return to Georgeham, his first marriage at an end, to live in the hut he had built in his two-acre field at Oxford Cross, named by him Ox's Cross, and begin to write the remarkable sequence of fifteen novels to which he gave the overall title, *A Chronical of Ancient Sunlight.*

In *The Village Book* and *The Labouring Life,* Henry wrote of Georgeham and its people with affection, with amusement, and sometimes with exasperation. Their ways were not his ways, and although he had become a countryman by choice, he remained an outsider, with a background, experiences, ideas and outlook on life far removed from those of his neighbours. *The Village Book* was prefaced with a disclaimer; it was 'an imaginative work which should not be read as the history of any particular village, and certainly not of any man or woman. Even the "I" and the "zur" and the "Mr Williamson" are but devices of story-telling'. However, in the preface to the American edition of *The Labouring Life,* Henry admitted that the characters were based on living people, although he accused himself of manipulating them, transforming them into Williamson characters for the purpose of fiction. Undoubtedly he did this to a certain extent, but each man, woman and child (his portrayals of children are amused and affectionate) depicted in these two books – under invented names – had a real existence in the Georgeham and Croyde of his day, and was recognisable to those who lived locally; a fact that caused a good deal of resentment when the portrait was not altogether favourable. Only a few, such as Muggy Smith, were happy, even eager, to be 'put in a book'.

Apart from the villagers, there is the recently arrived village constable, P.C. Bullcornworthy, whose real name was Corney, and who is caricatured as a conventional P.C. Plod. There are retired officers – Admiral Bampfylde, in reality Col. E. H. H. Elliott, D.S.O., of Pickwell Manor, and Col. Ponde, who was Captain Henry Bigge of Kittiwell in Croyde, who constructed a number of ornamental ponds in his garden. Both were members of the Parish Council, and appear in 'Cemetery or Burial Ground?', the account of the long series of acrimonious discussions, covering four years, which preceded a decision about an extension of the churchyard. There is Lady Maude Seeke (Miss Florence Hyde, of Croyde Bay House), who paid for the upkeep of the churchyard and beautified it with flowering plants. Finally there is the Rector, at that time the Revd Alfred Rose, who held the living of Georgeham from 1922 to 1930.

Yet in both books the principle character is the village itself. Henry liked to climb the church tower and gaze down on it. He ended *Life in a Devon Village* with a chapter called 'Surview and Farewell', presenting himself as standing on the tower recalling his first visit to Georgeham in May, 1914, and events of the ten years since his return after the First World War. Although he said that he wanted his record of village life to be as comprehensive as possible, and referred to himself earlier in the book as intending to be a 'serious historian of the village', the picture he has left of people and happenings is inevitably subjective and selective, lively though it is.

In that final chapter of *Life in a Devon Village* he showed his 1929 self preparing to leave the village for good – yet by the time the revised collection appeared in 1945, he had come back to spend the greater part of his remaining 32 years in or near Georgeham. (A cottage at Ilfracombe, bought in the 1960s, was an additional writing place during and after the failure of his second marriage.)

In *The Sawyers,* watching men topping the churchyard elms in 1924, he had written of the grave of an ex-soldier who had committed suicide and had been buried 'without a parson's blessing' under the trees. He had added 'When my time comes, I would like to be laid beside him'. When his time came, he was indeed buried in the old part of the churchyard, but near the west door, only a sparrow-flutter from the two cottages in which he had written the books that many readers still chose to regard as his best work, and for which, even now, he is probably best known.

10

A Time in the Village

Almost opposite the lych gate of Georgeham church is a cottage now called Churchsea, although until comparatively recently it was Chertsey. It has been suggested that the name was corrupted from church hay, and that what is now Chertsey House, just below, was once used as one of the small schools of the early 19th century – as was the Victoria Inn, now known as Millie's Cottage, on the corner opposite the King's Arms.

In 1923 my parents became tenants of Chertsey Cottage, and friends of Henry Williamson, who visited them often, usually late at night, to read aloud long passages of his early novels and nature stories.

For me, memories begin in that cottage, and with them a sense of the life of the village going on outside, separate from the life of my parents – who, like a number of others at that time, were incomers from elsewhere. Both were Devon-born, but both had been brought up as members of the non-affluent middle class – the son of a parson, the daughter of an unworldly architect and amateur inventor too unbusiness-like to make more than a very modest living. Yet this was enough to ensure that I was not sent to the village school, but went through the lych gate every morning and by way of the churchyard to the rectory, to spend three hours learning the three Rs and scraps of geography and history from the rector's wife, Mrs Rose.

Sometimes, looking down from my bedroom window, with its whorl of bottle glass in one pane (now gone). I watched the wild, revelling games of the village children. They scrabbled in the stream at the point where it disappeared under the road, ladling out water in old tin cans to throw at one another. They pushed wooden boxes on wheels up the hill and trundled triumphantly down while making noises conventionally taken to imitate one of the seldom-seen motor cars. They bowled iron hoops, shouted, fought, ran with tins on long strings trailing at heel. Just as there was never any question of my going to the village school, so there was never any question of my joining in these street games. If I had, everything about me would have marked me out as the outsider I was. It has been pointed out that what is called Standard English or Received Pronunciation is as much a dialect as any other dialect of Britain. My natural use of it would have been regarded as an absurd affectation. Their natural use of broad Devon might at first have been half-incomprehensible to me – and the fact that I would probably have picked it up quite quickly was just one of the reasons for my absurd – as it now seems – segregation.

So, solitary, but seldom consciously lonely, I made the little cottage garden my friend, and enjoyed going to the rectory, on the whole, and the excitement of finding that I could read. On weekly visits to Barnstaple for market day shopping, I had the big garden of St. Mary's Vicarage at the top of Fort Hill (later divided into two houses, Arisaig and Greengates) as a playground; as has been said, my grandfather was vicar of the parish now absorbed into that of St. Peter.

Then, at the end of four years in Chertsey Cottage, my world grew larger. In 1902 George Montague Style, a reputed millionaire, who already owned Spreacombe Manor, bought the Pickwell estate from Earl Fortescue, and almost completely rebuilt Pickwell Manor. Five years later he decided that it would be fitting for him to present Georgeham parish with a drill hall and miniature rifle range. A long, low building with a roof of red tiles was constructed on a site adjoining North Hole Farm, halfway between Georgeham and Forda. *Kelly's Directory* for 1910 shows that P. Moses was honorary secretary of the Georgeham and Croyde Rifle Club, North Hole. (In 1902 Philip Moses was the owner of Fig Tree Farm, but by 1906 he was landlord of the Manor House Hotel, as it was then called.)

The club evidently had a comparatively short life. By the beginning of the 1920s its premises had become a dwelling. The new owner was Miss Margaret Kemp-Welch, an artist who had exhibited at the Royal Academy, in the Paris Salon and in the provinces. (Her seemingly more accomplished elder sister Lucy was well known for her paintings of horses, dogs, flowers and landscapes.)^{Note 1}

Having bought the former drill hall she converted it into a bungalow, with a very large unceilinged room at one end to which she added a skylight; this became her studio. During her stay in Georgeham she painted murals in the chancel of Georgeham church, which were unveiled by the Bishop of Exeter in April, 1926, and a signboard for the village hall, built in 1926, at the instigation of Col. E.H.H. Elliot; an ex-Indian Army officer who had won the DSO in the First World War, and who by this time had become the owner of Pickwell.

Living alone, Miss Kemp-Welch may have found the long building too large for her; in 1927 my father bought it, and had two bedrooms taken out of the studio, which even then remained a big room. My mother renamed the bungalow Streamways. On the clay-cold November night of the day we moved in, I heard for the first time through an open window the rilling voice of the valley stream. Here, about two miles from its source on the hill running down from Oxford Cross, it poured over the lip of a fall some four feet high and ran down the gully that formed the northern boundary of the garden. Above the fall was the rickyard of the farm, with its carpet of old, rotted straw underfoot and the musty smell of last year's ricks. On the other side of the gully hedge was the farm orchard, full of little old leaning trees. Beyond the farm buildings, fields rose to the skyline.

From the garden the stream flowed along one side of a half-acre of level meadow; alders hung over it their purple catkins all winter and spring. Flag iris grew in the marshy ground, and reeds and ragged robin. At its lower end the meadow merged into the mud banks of a dam built to drive a dynamo to provide electricity for Forda House. The house had changed hands, and the new owner was indifferent to electric light; the waterwheel hung motionless and moss-grown and the dam was silting up.

Moorhens wandered up and down the valley, but seemed to prefer the banks of the dam as nesting places. When a brood hatched it sailed on the calm water, guarded by the hen, until the chicks were old enough to disperse; often from the orchard came the sound of their sharp questioning 'Cher-rek? Cher-rek?'

From the little meadow a field like a section of an amphitheatre swept upwards, sheltered on its western side by a copse of oaks. Above the copse was a patch of furze, forming the crown of the hill. From there one could see the whole valley; the softly-moulded hills and their pattern of fields; the little wood of beeches at Oxford Cross; Georgeham with the road running down from it, and the widening valley where Croyde lay half-hidden by tall elms, and the dunes beyond, through which the stream flowed to the sea. From the church tower, half a mile away, ringers' practise, hated during the years at Chertsey Cottage when it was close and loud, sounded mellow across the fields.

On this hilltop bracken had rooted among the grass, and there were little spaces of rabbit-bitten turf peppered with droppings. Honeysuckle climbed over the hawthorn bushes in the hedge bordering this patch; foxgloves and bluebells flowered in May. It became a place in which to lie hidden for hours, watching kestrels hover and drop like stones, or buzzards swing over the valley (once, just once, a pair nested in the oak copse), or gulls drift down the sky at evening, floating on the air with unmoving wings, or swallows sweeping across the hillsides.

On fine Sunday evenings during the light months it was as though the populations of the two villages were changing places. Young couples, whole families, groups of youths, and couples pushing prams went up or down the valley road. They went to visit friends and relations, to the young men's club, to church or just to walk for the pleasure of it. For many, in those years, it was the only time of real freedom in the whole week, the few hours of absolute leisure. Motorized traffic was almost non-existent on Sundays. They could stroll at ease, gossiping, between the green contours of their familiar valley.

Sometimes great elm-felling gales roared up from the Atlantic. Set back fifty yards from the road an almost continuous line of elms began at North Hole Farm and ran to within a short distance of Croyde. Tall, magnificent trees, perhaps over a century old, they were shallow rooted like all their species, and from time to time one or two would be brought down by a gale. The remainder did not survive to become victims of Dutch Elm disease; they were felled for their timber during the war, and the sight of their white stumps when I came back after absence struck like a blow, as did the ripped-out hedges and ploughed-up hilltop above the oak copse.

For a single day, without warning, the valley stream changed its nature – not in winter, which would have been understandable, but just before midsummer. On June 6th, 1931, it was grey from first light. At about seven o'clock it began to rain heavily out of a sky like wet slate. There was no ordinary storm atmosphere: no lightning flashes or thunder. It was impossible to guess what was causing the threatening sky, which seemed to press lower and lower over the hillside. Crystal rods of rain flailed the ground. Suddenly the wall of the barn on the edge of the rickyard burst out, washed by a rolling wave of water that swept on its crest the farm cart that had been standing in the barn. The stream gully was full of water which began to rise towards the house. We rescued our dogs from their kennel outside, and waited. How high would it come?

There was no need to worry. In an hour or two the rain eased, and the water slowly ebbed, revealing that it had made one saddening change to the course of our stretch of the stream: it had destroyed the little waterfall below the rickyard, carrying away the big stones that had formed it and scattering them along the stream bed. The farm cart lay in the little meadow beyond our boundary, on its side, amid a layer of straw, cabbages, small branches, dead chickens, rags, old saucepans and empty cans.

The following Thursday the *North Devon Journal* devoted almost a page to the flood, with photographs. It had sent a reporter, Cedric Foulkes, to survey the damage. He chose to ride to Braunton (where the road was knee-deep in water rushing down from the direction of Heddon Mill along the swollen river Caen) and on to Georgeham by way of St. Brannock's Hill, which resembled a river bed, with hummocks of mud and large stones making every yard hazardous. The road had been sluiced to its foundations in some places, and in others was half blocked by collapsed hedges. Georgeham was described as 'a stricken village of gloom and sorrow'. A farmer at Spreacombe told Cedric Foulkes that there had been a cloudburst at 'Roddaway', in other words Roadway, the highest point of Pickwell Down. From there the water had rushed down to swell the little dam built by a previous rector to provide power for electric light, broken the dam wall and flooded the rectory. The Revd Sharples explained that he had come downstairs into almost waist-deep water, opened the front door to let it escape and been swept outside. Unable to reopen the door, he had climbed in again by a window. Some of the furniture in the lower rooms had been washed through the French windows on to the gravel drive. All the cottages in the lower part of the village had inevitably found their ground floors half-full of muddy water.

Sweeping on down the valley, the rushing water had strewed its flotsam across the meadows. In Croyde, all the cottages alongside the stream were flooded; of the two villages, this one probably suffered the most.

Compared with many floods – especially, for instance, with the Lynmouth flood of 1952 – this was a mild affair; there was no loss of life, and only a few animals died. Yet its sudden violence, on a June day, ensured that it was remembered and talked about for years.

11

Leaving the Village

In May, 1937, a newcomer arrived in Georgeham, a slim, dark, athletic looking man, with something mercurial about him; he moved quickly and decisively and gave the impression of an eager interest in life, an interest that is reflected in the book he soon began to write, his appreciative account of the Georgeham of those years, *Home in Ham*.

He was R.W. Thompson, always known as Tommy. A busy freelance journalist, he had also published half a dozen books, accounts of adventurous years spent in Argentina and Australia. His wife, Pat, was a successful dress designer; they had three small children, Patricia Ann, aged five, Thomas Patrick, aged three, and Maria Blanche, a year old, all known by nicknames: Topsy, Thompo and Beany-Bird respectively. Tommy had evidently met Henry Williamson at some time during the past year or two (which may be why he chose to move to Georgeham): he recorded that 'Henry Williamson by calling me always Thompo had fixed the name for Thomas Patrick by chance'.[Note 1]

Tommy enquired for a cottage to let. As he wrote in *Home in Ham* 'In a corner of the village, tucked under a gently sloping hillside, there was a cottage. White roses climbed the porch and hung in clusters veiling the door, and there was a crown of roses above the garden gate. Masses of valerian sprang from the stone garden wall that buttressed the hillside against the road – for the garden sloped upwards above the level of the roof'.

This was, once again, Vale House. After my grandmother's death in 1935, it had become the property of my father. It had had one or two short-term tenants but was now on the market. However, Tommy rented it, and he and his family lived there until the end of September, when they moved to Kentisbury Cottage, at the east end of the village. During the months in Vale House, Tommy had at first taken over as his workplace the room above the garage that Henry Williamson had used during the years 1925 to 1929. However, the arrival of a succession of friends on holiday meant that 'the little garden-room upstairs became a bedroom, and that was that'.

The rector, the Revd Harry Sharples, who had shown Tommy 'great friendliness, his quick eyes smiling' and 'looked out old papers which have helped me greatly to find the beginnings of Ham', had also given him permission to use a room in the big stone-built stables (later to be converted to the dwellings which exist today) as a place where he could write in absolute seclusion. In return, Tommy wrote 'The Church of St. George, Georgeham, an Appreciation and brief description', an eight-page booklet which was soon on sale in the church, price twopence.

Tommy had begun *Home in Ham* during his early days at Vale House, but set it aside to concentrate on other writing; in particular his novel based on the life of Juan de Rosas, *Portrait of a Patriot.* He took it up again on board ship: three months after they settled in at Kentisbury Cottage, Tommy and Pat were sailing to South America. Tommy was planning a book which would become *Voices in the Wilderness,* 'a record of my search for El Dorado and of those who have sought and found new lives'. He hoped to identify a stretch of territory on the Alto Para that would attract British colonists.

He worked on *Home in Ham* during both the outward and homeward voyages and, once back in Georgeham, went on with it with his usual speed, so that it was finished by September, 1938, and published – equally speedily – by the end of the year.

A restless man, who had already moved house half a dozen times since his marriage, he tried to persuade himself that he would spend the rest of his life in Georgeham. 'Strangely I did not ever seem to myself a visitor in Georgeham. I lived there, and if anyone asked (as they sometimes did) "How long are you staying?" I answered with dignity "I'm not staying. This is my home". In my usual manner, I felt I would always live there, but that simply meant that I was content.'

Though much of *Home in Ham* is taken up with accounts of such activities as net fishing from Putsborough beach at night with Alec Brown, Alwyne Willis, Jackal, or Jacko, Bourchier and Alf Tucker, sailing with Captain Chichester aboard his Braunton ketch *Enid,* exploring the Spreacombe iron mines or the great cave on Baggy with Alwyne Willis, and visiting the boxing booth at Barnstaple Fair with Charlie Ovey (as Henry Williamson had done more than a dozen years earlier) he included many sketches of villages, using their real names, having no fear of causing resentment, as all his portraits were kindly.

The outbreak of war ensured that Tommy's stay in Georgeham was over in little more than two years. He became a war correspondent and, after the war, married again, fathered more children, and wrote ten books all connected in some way with the war, including two biographies of Churchill and two of Montgomery. Yet of all his books – some two dozen altogether – *Home in Ham* stands out as the most carefree, from the first sentence, 'We are happy in Ham, my wife, Topsy, Thompo, Beany-Bird, and I' to the last, 'It is good to be home in Ham'.

Even before the war began, the north-west corner of Devon had been chosen as the site of an RAF station. In 1934 a small aerodrome and flying club opened on land that had previously been Chivenor Farm. This, and the adjoining Marsh Farm, were taken over by the Air Ministry, and converted to an air base, originally for Coastal Command. From the time it opened in July, 1940, it was to play an important part in what soon became known as the Battle of the Atlantic, when convoys suffered increasingly destructive attacks from U-boats operating virtually without hindrance from bases around the French coast. For two years, from April, 1942, two squadrons of Wellington bombers flew dozens of sorties down to the Bay of Biscay, destroying many U-boats. Beaufighter squadrons were also stationed at Chivenor in 1941 to intercept Junkers 88s and Fokker-Wolf 200s attacking British shipping. The airfield attracted hostile attention: on March 31st, 1941, a Heinkel dropped bombs on the railway at Wrafton, and during April there were two raids. In the first a Junker 88 bombed and machine-gunned buildings and in the second four Heinkels caused considerable damage to aircraft, buildings and runways. In November of that year a Junkers landed on the main runway; its crew were under the impression that they had arrived in France. They were taken prisoner, and their aircraft was transferred to the Royal Aeronautical Establishment at Farnborough for a thorough examination. When two Heinkels crash-landed on Lundy, their crews were initially taken to Chivenor for questioning.

In Ilfracombe, a number of hotels were commandeered by the army, and the Warwick Office of the Royal Army Pay corps arrived to spend the next five years or so in the town. Most of the hotels became billets for soldiers and members of the ATS, but the uncarpeted rooms of the Ilfracombe Hotel itself (demolished in 1976) were soon full of clerks in khaki working at trestle table desks.

To guard against the possibility of German landings, hundreds of tall posts were driven into the beaches of Saunton, Croyde and Woolacombe. It was as though the Sunken Forest that once filled part of Barnstaple Bay had arisen from the sea and taken possession the foreshore. Even in wartime, some people came for holidays to Croyde, and at high tide, a bather might climb to the top of a submerged post, looking like a person about to walk upon the water.

In the autumn of 1943 the area became a military training ground. The Woolacombe Bay Hotel was chosen as the headquarters of the United States Assault Training Centre. A brass plate at the entrance to the hotel records that on the beaches of Woolacombe and Saunton, the American Troops who were to spearhead landings on Normandy beaches codenamed Omaha and Utah 'underwent the rigorous and specialised training which enabled them with their British and Canadian comrades in arms to achieve a decisive and historic victory on 6th June, 1944'. A memorial dedicated exclusively to the American soldiers was unveiled as recently as May, 1992, by the 82 year-old American officer who commanded the Centre, Brigadier General Paul W. Thompson. It stands on the grassy strip between Woolacombe Esplanade and the edge of the cliffs, and takes the form of two tall slim shafts of granite, each with one face finely polished.

Not surprisingly, a number of girls from the north-west corner of Devon became GI brides, and those whose husbands survived the war left for a new life in America.

Away on war service, coming home only on brief leaves, I saw little of the valley villages after 1939. By the summer of 1943 Streamways

was sold. While they waited to move to a new home in Plymouth, my parents looked about for a cottage to rent. At the western end of Georgeham, opposite what was then called the Village Institute, not the Village Hall, stood the forge, a whitewashed building with a cottage alongside and partly above it. It belonged to the smith, but he lived in a house nearby. My parents became its temporary tenants.

A flight of stone steps led up from the road under a peak of tiles that linked the outhouse kitchen on the left with the main building. A big rainwater butt stood at one side of the door, which opened directly into the living room. Behind the butt was a small dark cave that contained an Elsan. Apart from the kitchen there were four rooms, three up and one down; each had a small window divided into twelve panes. In two of the upstairs rooms a pane was missing and replaced by a piece of cardboard; a chunk of plaster had fallen from one ceiling, revealing the laths. Several walls showed cracks. In his own time, one of the village masons carried out repairs.

The kitchen was built into the hillside. Pallid ivy shoots thrust through chinks in the slates overhead, and the rough stones of the inner walls were silvered with the trails of snails every morning. There was no water laid on and therefore no sink. Washing up and clothes washing had to be done in enamel bowls and zinc tubs, and the water thrown away in the little patch of grass around the kitchen roof, reached by another flight of steps.

From the window of the kitchen we could look down Netherham Hill. At its foot, then, stood a working pump, which served all the cottages on the west side of the village. We saw people carrying buckets and ewers to fetch water, and staggering up the steep hill after filling them. Twice a day we went for our own supply, taking a bucket or three gallon watering can. The pump threw a good head of water, but in jerky gouts, slopping and wasting on the stones. We used water frugally, far more so than we did at Chertsey Cottage twenty years earlier, when our drinking water was brought to the door from our landlady's house, the stream was near and the slope less steep to climb with full buckets.

The smith lighted his fire soon after seven each morning, and by eight o'clock we would hear the bell-like chime of hammer on metal. Often a big farm horse stood outside, waiting to be shod. Strict petrol rationing meant that there were fewer cars on the rural roads than there had been since the 1920s, and carters and farmers were glad to have retained their horses. All items of furniture from Streamways not going into store, had been transported to the cottage in a horse-drawn cart.

Even so, there was no longer enough work to keep the smith busy all day. On the tarred half-door of the forge he wrote 'Please Come Mornings'; about noon he closed the doors and went home for the day. He was a sergeant in the Home Guard, which paraded every Sunday morning outside the Village Institute. No. 27 Platoon of A Company of the 25th Ilfracombe Battalion of the Home Guard had 38 members in 1944, and a photograph of them was taken by the Barnstaple photographer, R.L. Knight, in September of that year. We saw them arriving one by one, familiar figures transformed for a few hours into uniformed men. Their leather anklets were well polished and their uniforms were neat, but their bearing was casual and non-military.

The Company commander arrived in his car, for which he was granted petrol; he parked it outside the Institute and went in. If there was to be a lecture the sergeant in charge marched the platoon inside in single file; if there was to be an exercise or target practise the officer took over, and the platoon marched away. It reappeared after church-goers' cars had gone, and was dismissed on the roadside opposite the forge.

Behind the patch of grass above the kitchen roof was a big field of barley. Many fields around the village that had been pasture were planted with corn; oats had a silvery sheen and barley a tinge of red, and sunset painted them riper than at noon. Almost for the last time, as the war came to an end, the crops were cut by horse power, using old-fashioned reaper-and-binders.

I spent only a short time in the cottage, seeing it at its best in the weeks of a late summer leave. But looking back, it remains a useful reminder of the drudgery that was commonplace for country people – especially country women – in the centuries before the provision of mains services that are now taken for granted in the industralized countries.

12

Life Savers and Warning Lights

etween the headlands of Hartland and Morte lie some
eighteen miles of often wild water; mapmakers identify it as
'Barnstaple or Bideford Bay', having regard to the partisan
feelings of the rival towns. Similarly they usually mark the bar at the
mouth of the Taw-Torridge estuary as Barnstaple or Bideford Bar',
although it sometimes appears simply as Bideford Bar. The bay, and
the bar, must have taken the lives of hundreds of seamen over the
centuries. In the days of sail, a storm might drive half a dozen little
wooden vessels ashore on the long sand beaches of Saunton, Croyde
or Woolacombe in a single day or night. Unlike the rocky cliffs, the
sand offered some possibility of survival to any crew swept ashore,
but even so there were drownings in the heavy surf. As late as the
1930s, the jagged timbers of one or two of the wrecks were still to be
seen jutting from the sand.

The first aid to safer navigation for ships approaching the estuary
mouth was a lighthouse at Crow Point, built in 1822, with a high light
90 feet above sea level and low light 48 feet above high water. A tide
ball is shown on the 1891 Ordnance map about 400 yards to the west;
this could be raised or lowered to indicate to shipping when it was
safe to cross the bar. A third light, known as Blinking Billy, flashed
red and yellow lights alternately.

In spite of all this, there were still many wrecks. In 1930 a writer recorded that a former shipping agent at Appledore had compiled a list of ships lost between Hartland and Baggy during the years 1799 to 1858: one man-of-war (HMS Weazel, evidently), ten schooners, sixteen brigs, 22 sloops, a Queen's cutter, a packet cutter, two yachts and nine other unspecified vessels.Note 1 Until the RNLI was founded in 1824, no national lifeboat service existed, although by the beginning of the 19th century a number of English coastal towns, including Plymouth and Exmouth, had some kind of rescue craft, and in 1815 the customs officer at Ilfracombe, Thomas Rodd, suggested that a lifeboat should be available in the harbour. By 1822 the Lysons were able to note that three large skiffs cruised off Ilfracombe 'in the winter season for the express purpose of assisting vessels in distress'.Note 2

Growing concern at the number of losses in Barnstaple Bay led to the provision of a lifeboat, *Volunteer*, at Appledore in 1825. Six years later the newly founded founded North Devon Humane Society replaced her with a six-oared boat appropriately named *Assistance*. She saved more than twenty lives during the next fifteen years, but was moved to Airy Point, on the north shore of the estuary, so that she could be launched directly into the Bay, using teams of horses from nearby farms. (For two years she was apparently left in the open – perhaps covered by a tarpaulin – but in 1848 a lifeboat house was built in an inlet in the dunes about a mile north of the lighthouse.) According to Samuel Ellacott, Farmer Hernaman of West Saunton Farm always strove to get his horses to the shore first, in the charge of his horseman, George Coates. Ten horses, all with riders, towed the lifeboat to the water on a wheeled carriage, tracks being attached to enable it to cross the soft sand of the foreshore. The tracks were then removed, and two lines of five horses drew the boat into water deep enough for it to float clear. The procedure was reversed when the lifeboat returned, and once she had been pulled to the entrance to her house, the horses were taken round to the back to haul her up the ramp by means of a steel cable.Note 3

Successors to *Assistance* were *Dolphin*, given by the RNLI in 1857, and several larger, self-righting boats – *George and Catherine* in 1866, presented by Mr and Mrs George Jeremy, and finally three boats in succession, all named *Robert and Catherine* and all given by a Miss Leicester of Bayswater, in 1881, 1902 and 1912.

A pamphlet, 'The Wreck on Saunton Sands', by Mary Hartley, describes, in some 150 lines of blank verse, the rescue of the six-man crew of a ship driven ashore at Saunton in November, 1864. The particular interest of this is not in the verse, which is conventionally sentimental and pious, but in extracts from the 'Journal of the National Life-boat Institution' and some introductory notes by the author.

Despite the fact that she was then living in Bideford, Mary Hartley collected money to provide a life-boat, named after her, which was stationed at Broughton Ferry, near Dundee. She also collected 'nearly the whole cost of the Braunton new Life-boat House', the Institution's 'Journal' notes. Writing from Victoria Terrace, Exeter, in 1865, she remarked that 'In the early part of last year a life-boat house and a room attached thereto for resuscitation, with every comfort, was built on piles on these Sands. One of the first gales of winter brought a distressing proof of the necessity of such a provision, and which suggested to the writer this poem,'. She added that all profits from the sale of her pamphlet were to go to the Lifeboat Institution, and dedicated it to the branches of the RNLI at Dundee, Braunton and Barnstaple, signing herself 'their faithful coadjutor and humble servant'.

The wreck that Mrs Hartley wrote about was of the schooner the *Meridian*. She stranded near the lifeboat house, and the lifeboat was soon launched, but 'owing to the intervening sandbank, she could not get to the vessel. The ship-wrecked crew were, however, subsequently taken ashore in a very exhausted condition, especially the poor cabinboy. They were at once conveyed to the Resuscitation Room attached to the Life-boat House, and there treated in accordance with the new Instructions for the Restoration of the Apparently Drowned, recently issued by the Royal National Life-boat Institution. The poor boy would, no doubt, have died but for these valuable means. He and the crew, however, happily recovered.'

There seems to be no way of knowing whether the new life-boat house, with its useful extra room, was built on the site of the original house of 1848. Its position in 1886, when the Ordnance Survey 6 inch to the mile map published in 1890 was surveyed, is roughly a mile from the lighthouse towards Saunton Down. However, it was never an easy station to maintain, and sand erosion brought about its closure in 1919, its crew having saved 85 lives.

The lighthouse at Crow Point had a longer life. It was replaced in

1959 by a girder light, but that too was removed some years later.

The estuary itself seems always to have been a hazardous place for ships in the days of sail, and especially for rowing boats. As has been said, Ogilby's map of 1675 shows that there must have been a regular ferry from a point not far from the ancient chapel of St. Anne (until comparatively recently, the solitary house about a mile from Crow Point, later known as the White House and as Crow Beach House, was the Ferry House.) St. Anne's was one of the five chapels belonging to the medieval parish of Braunton. and it can hardly be doubted that it was built for the spiritual comfort of travellers; the southbound could offer prayers for their safety before taking the ferry, and the northbound could give thanks after landing. St. Anne, like St. Nicholas, was a patron saint of sailors.

Tristram Risdon, writing in the mid-17th century, may have seen the chapel; he had certainly heard of it. 'Solitarily situated is St. Anne's Chapel, and very near the sea, yet doubts not drowning, so much as the swallowing up of the Sands, driven by the Drifts of the North-West-Wind, stirring Storms, and playing the Tyrant in this Tract. Hereby is the Union of the two notable Rivers of the Towridge and Taw, that Hand in Hand with mutual Affection slip into the Sea'.

The dissolution of chantry chapels in the mid-16th century probably caused the chapel to be abandoned. It seems to have fallen into ruin fairly gradually. A number of guidebooks of the second half of the 19th century mention it. As one writer, in about 1845, observed that 'not far from the Lighthouse are the walls of an old building called St. Anne's chapel' it must then have lost no more than its roof.[Note 4] Fifty years later, someone else claimed that 'unfortunately stones were wanted to build a cowshed; the ruins were "handy" and – they disappeared. Until quite recently some remains were still to be traced, but now even they have vanished'. Despite this, he must have seen foundations, as he stated that the chapel measured fourteen feet six inches by twelve feet.[Note 5]

However, it seems that something did remain. The writer H.M. Tomlinson, many of whose books were widely read during the earlier part of the 20th century, visited Appledore in 1917. He was 44 years old, and had served as a war correspondent since 1914; he was probably sick of writing of the sights and sounds of war. He came back to England to become literary editor of the 'Nation and Athenaeum'. Several of his essays, published in a collection called

Old Junk in 1925, describe the Appledore area, without naming it, and its ships and seamen. One is simply called 'The Dunes'.

'The dunes are another world. They are two miles across the uncertain and hazardous tides of the estuary. The folk of the village never go over. The dunes are nothing. They are the horizon . . . (they) tremble in the broad flood of wind, light and sea, diaphanous and fading, always on the limit of vision, the point of disappearing . . . It was a perverse tide on a windless day that drifted me over'. Landing, he felt that 'this country would not be on the map'; he was breaking into 'what was still the first day', even though he saw an old beam of a ship, harsh with barnacles, lying at the foot of the first slope. He began to make his way into the dunes, and 'got into a hollow which had a floor of hoary lichen, with bronze hummocks of moss . . . Just showing in the drift on the seaward side of them were some worked stones and a little brickwork. When the sandhill paused, it had almost covered a building where man once worshipped. I could find nobody afterwards who remembered the church, or had even heard of it'. He thought the valley looked very well as it was, with a blue flower (probably Viper's Bugloss) growing on one of the stones of the forgotten altar.[Note 6]

By that time another chapel of St Anne had been in existence for over twenty years. The Christie Trustees gave land for it almost opposite the entrance to the Saunton Golf Club, and provided stone from their quarry on the side of Saunton Down. It was intended as the chancel of a larger church, at a time when it was expected that the area around it would see rapid development. Happily nothing came of this, although a number of houses, and the original Saunton Sands Hotel, were constructed a few years later along the low cliffs nearby.

Carpeted in deep blue, its interior is small and simple. Its visitors' book shows that many people come here, and are moved by what they find. In the east window, the central light of three shows St. Anne cradling a sailing ship in her arms. Doves fly about her, each with a ring, her symbol, in its beak. She stands on a sandhill, with Viper's Bugloss growing at her feet. Below, against a background of sea and fishing boats, is an imaginary depiction of the ancient chapel in the dunes. In the left light, St Agnes with her lamb and sword of martyrdom, wearing a robe embroidered with lilies, stands in a flowery meadow; in the right, St John is seen on the island of Patmos, at work on the Apocalypse. In the north wall is a small memorial window, coloured in delicate blues, green and yellows, to Herbert Leonard Hustwayte, 'priest of this parish' (he was curate from 1967 until his death in 1978). Its counterpart in the south wall is to his wife, Coralie, who died a year before him. Both show animals, birds and flowers to be found on the Burrows.

A well-kept lawn surrounds the chapel and a shallow hollow, grown with bracken, young sycamores and wild clematis, divides it from the road. The notes provided for the information of visitors are headed 'The Chapel in the Bracken'. In the porch is a roughly-hewn stone basin, said to be the font of the old dune chapel – yet why should baptisms have been solemnized in so remote a place?

13

Lovers of the Dunes

Until the early 19th century, Braunton and Saunton were spelled Branton and Santon. 'Santon is in the parish of Branton, not inaptly so termed by the Sand that hath overblown many hundred Acres of Land' wrote Risdon. 'And near this Hamlet, the Country-People had so undermined a Hill of Sand, by digging into it to carry it to their Grounds, that a great quantity thereof fell down, discovering the top of a Tree, which, by further Search, was found to be 30 feet in length. So that it plainly appeareth, this Circuit of Marsh-Land (now of Sands over-blowing, called the Burrows) was in elder ages stored with Woods and tall Timber-Trees'.

In view of this evidence that the dunes were called the Burrows long before 1809, when the first Ordnance maps were prepared under the direction of Lieut. Mudge, in the Tower of London, on behalf of the army authorities, it is surprising that the map for Devon marks them as Braunton *Barrows,* and puts in a Barrow House just halfway along the old road from Saunton Court to the ferry, at a point where it was joined by a lane from Lobb. The map published in London by G. and J. Cary in 1821 again marks *Barrow* House, although it shows Braunton *Burrows.* However, the explanation may be that at one time the words 'barrow' and 'burrow' seem to have been used more or less interchangeably in the west country.

Risdon's contemporary, Thomas Westcote, also spoke of 'Santon, having the adjunct of court, as where a lord's court was kept; it taketh the name of the situation which joineth near the sea, on a large sandy strand, whence in the ebb the wind drives the sand abundantly to huge heaps near the house, from which is daily fetched great quantity to manure the neighbouring fields, and yet never emptied or lessened, but continually again supplied by the wind; so therefore called Santon, quasi Sand-Town'. The house he mentions may have been Barrow House, or an earlier house on the same site; it can hardly have been the 17th century Saunton Court since, like today's building, that would have stood at some distance from the Burrows.

Hidden from the road, with the great grassy curve of Lankham Combe sweeping up to the skyline on its northern side, the present Saunton Court stands in a sheltered, almost secret place. Did the first Saxon to come to this area choose to build himself a dwelling there for that reason? It may well have been the home of the former owner of the Manor of Saunton, Dodo or Dodda, when the Norman Tetbald, or Theobald Fitzberners, dispossessed him.

In the 16th century Saunton Court was the property of a branch of the Chichester family. In 1545 Sir Robert Chichester owned a small late medieval rubble stone manor house with cross wings and a two-storeyed porch. Almost a century later it belonged to Sir John Luttrell. It seems to have remained of modest size, virtually a farmhouse (it was in fact occupied by a farming family from Braunton named Tucker in the late 19th early 20th century) until 1932, when the then owner employed Sir Edwin Lutyens to remodel and extend it.[Note 1] With Sir Guy Dawber, Lutyens carried out the work at a reputed cost of £55,000. Lutyens kept the old porch, with its round-headed arch, as well as the tall twelve-pane sash windows in the hall, but made internal changes, and added a service court on the left of the main wing. Characteristically, having enhanced the house, he turned his attention to the garden. A lawn was laid out in front of the house, with a higher terrace at the side, reached by his favourite convex-concave steps. Gate piers topped by stone balls flanked steps down to a lower terrace, with a water channel flowing from a semi-circular grotto with a goat's head gargoyle; beyond this was a circular pool.[Note 2]

In the 11th century there may have been more signs of the 'Woods and tall Timber-Trees' that once grew across much of what is now Barnstaple (or Bideford) Bay. A large tract of submerged forest was

92

uncovered after a storm near Northam Burrows in 1864. Townsend Hall recorded seeing the stems of between 70 and 80 large trees, chiefly oak, ash, birch and hazel, broken off about two feet above the peat bed. Flint and other instruments were found, as well as the antlers of red deer and the bones of Celtic short-horned oxen, horses, sheep and men. Even in comparatively recent times, very low tides have revealed tree stumps.[Note 3]

Writers of guide books in the Edwardian era seemed to have regarded the Burrows as of little interest to visitors in general. One simply called them 'a mile-wide waste, only interesting to the botanist'.[Note 4] Another conceded that 'the wild, waste tract of rolling sandhills, blown up from the sea' was 'not all barren by any means, for they are bounded together by a coarse grass, have a rich and peculiar flora, and yield to the entomologist some of his special prizes.'[Note 5] However, the Ward, Lock guide to Barnstaple which came out in 1905 was more appreciative. 'This is a very popular resort with Barnstaple. The sands are most extensive, and skirt the Braunton Burrows, where there are good golf links. There is a fine walk along the sands to Braunton Lighthouse. In addition to the interest always attaching to a lighthouse, there is the further reward of a charming view. On the left in the far distance can be seen busy Barnstaple, and flowing from thence the wide river Taw; that is to say, wide if the tide be high, but narrow and showing innumerable sandbanks at low water'. Having noted Instow and Appledore on the far shore, the writer adds, 'For returning from the lighthouse, the path leads back to Braunton or Wrafton railway station – the latter is actually nearer (4 miles)'. Carriages could be hired at Braunton station. There were said to be several lodging houses, and the original Saunton Hotel, forerunner of the much larger building constructed in 1932, was already in existence.

The golf links had been established in 1897 as a nine-hole course. (Today the Saunton Golf Club has two 18-hole courses.) Entrance fee and annual subscription were both a guinea, and there was a weekly charge of 7s 6d. By 1908 Devon had more than two dozen golf-courses, though the majority were of only 9 holes.[Note 6] Most, like Saunton, were literally 'links', in the dictionary sense of 'level or undulating sandy ground near the sea shore, with turf and coarse grass; ground on which golf is played, often resembling that of preceding sense'.

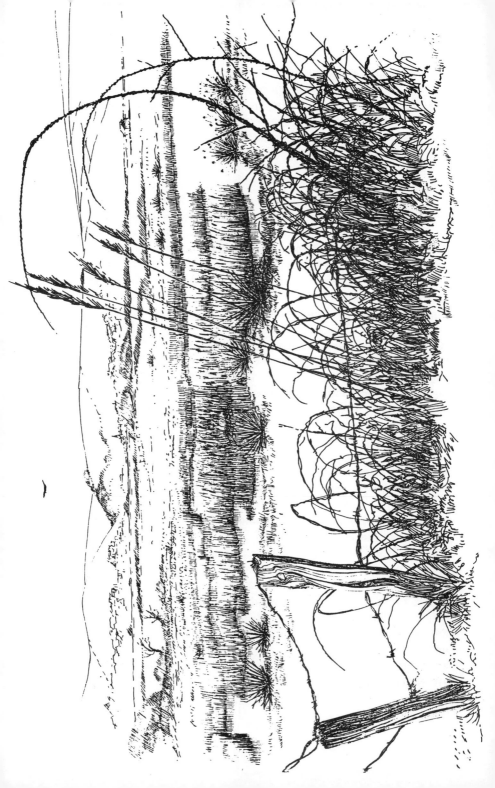

In his *Last Diary* – which, like his better known *The Journal of a Disappointed Man,* appeared under the name W.N.P. Barbellion – a young Barnstaple-born naturalist, Bruce Cummings, headed an entry dated January 1919, 'The Cottage on the Shore'. 'It was as myst-erious as Stevenson's 'Pavilion on the Links'. For a long time I never noticed any indication of its being inhabited, save a few chickens at the back which no one seemed to feed. I could see it from miles around, as it was situated in a desolate, treeless waste, thousands of acres of marshes and duckponds (known as the Mires) on the one side, and on the other a wilderness of sandy links and sandhills swarming with rabbits (known as the Burrows). Immediately in front, the waters of a broad tidal estuary came up almost to the door during spring tides. The nearest habitation was the lighthouse, a mile away round the corner on the sand near the harbour's bar'. At last, on a spring day, the diarist saw through binoculars a man come out of the cottage and throw some corn to the chickens, but by the time he had walked to the cottage, the man had disappeared. Time passed, 'and I began to think he had been an hallucination . . . Then one day I ran up against him on the Mires, and we exchanged greetings. He was a round, tubby, short man with a stubble of beard. Devon folk would have called him bungy, stuggy . . . We discussed birds (he was the gamekeeper) and became fast friends. He would take me on the round of his duckponds, and sometimes he sent me a postcard when there were wild swans or geese "in over", or when he had discovered a "stranger" on his water'. Barbellion did not suspect the presence of a woman in the cottage until, in search of the gamekeeper, he visited it and knocked on the door. After a pause he heard 'long preparatory noises, as if someone were climbing up from an underground cellar or cave, or wandering down a long, dark passage. Bolts were drawn (and powerful enough they sounded to make fast a portcullis) and I watched the door opening with curiosity; a tall, fat, middle-aged woman stood there blinking at me like an owl unaccustomed to daylight. Her eyes were weak blue, and her face puffy and red.

"Oh, is Fedder about?" I enquired.

Without changing a muscle of her face, she replied mechanically: "No, but Fedder said if the young gentleman called, I was to say that the shovellers brought off their brood all right."

Barbellion thanked her and left, hearing her bolt the door again. He wondered what the woman did in the desolate cottage, and decided

that 'she did nothing, thought nothing, perhaps only feared a little, so she always bolted the door and hid herself away. I suppose if one saw nothing bigger than a kingplover or a seagull during the twelve months, and heard no noises other than the trumpet of wild swans and the cries of Fedder's wild fowl, a tall man six feet high, with a voice like a human being's, must seem a little disconcerting.'

The cottage was of course then still known as the Ferry House.

Towards the end of the *Last Diary*, Barbellion remembered the Burrows again: 'The dunes are always associated in my mind with burning hot, cloudless summer days, during the whole long course of which without ceasing Lapwings flopped around my head, uttering their crazy wails, circuses of scimitar-winged Swifts swished by and screamed hysterically, the face of the blue sky was dotted at regular intervals with singing Larks, singing all day long without intermittence, poised menacingly overhead, so that the white hot needle-points of their song seemed likely at any moment to descend perpendicularly and penetrate the skull . . . Just here at my feet is an avalanche, jagged boulders of silica are descending and spreading out in a fan-shaped talus—only sand grains, so I cannot hear the crash of the boulders, but matter-atomic solar systems – colossal!

And behind all, behind every sight and every other sound, is the sound of the great sea, the all-powerful creator of the dunes . . . Superficially all seems dead and dull. Reflection brings the deeper understanding of myriad forms of life, creeping, running, springing, burrowing – of noisy, screaming, struggling life, dominated by the august, secular movements of the great sea.

Sometimes, towards the end of the afternoon, I would grow tired, the brilliance would become garish. Then, leaving the thyme, the eyebright, the wild pansies, the viper's bugloss (in clusters), an occasional teazle, after boxing every sort of insect and every sort of plant that I had not collected before, I would hurry out to the shore, take off my clothes, and be rebaptised by the sea'.

Bruce Frederick Cummings was born in Barnstaple in 1889. He recorded that he chose his pen name, Barbellion, when he saw it over a shop window in London and was struck by its 'fine truculent ring'. As for the initials, he explained – no doubt more than half jokingly – that they stood for 'Wilhelm Nero Pilate, three of the greatest failures in history'. He was the youngest of a family of three boys and three girls. Their father, John Cummings, was a journalist in charge of the local office of the *Devon and Exeter Gazette*; he loved his work, and determined that his sons should also become journalists. In the case of the two older boys – Arthur, later to become well known in Fleet Street as A.J. Cummings, and Harry, who worked for years as Parliamentary Correspondent of what was then the *Manchester Guardian* – this was no hardship. But from his earliest years, Bruce had little interest in anything but zoology, and in particular marine biology. As a boy in his 'teens, he began to contribute to the *Zoologist,* and an elderly naturalist who called at his home and asked to see the writer of an essay that had interested him was astonished to find himself talking to a schoolboy.

Compelled by his father to sign articles apprenticing him to journalism at the age of seventeen, Bruce Cummings vowed to work 'frantically' during the next five years in the hope that by the time he was 22 he could find himself some kind of natural history appointment. Astonishingly, entirely self-taught, and in competition with university graduates, he succeeded; in October, 1911, he came first in an examination to fill a position as an assistant at the Natural History Museum, South Kensington.

He married in 1915 and his only child, a daughter, was born the following year. It was not until after his marriage that he learned the reason for the constant ill-health that had troubled him for a number of years: he had multiple sclerosis. (His wife had been told this by his doctor before the wedding, and insisted that it made no difference to her decision.)

Increasing disability forced Cummings to resign his post at the Museum in 1917, and he died two years later at the age of 30.

It was a great happiness to him that he had lived long enough to see his *Journal* published, and to prepare his *Last Diary* and a collection of essays, *Enjoying Life,* for publication, although they appeared posthumously.

Like Henry Williamson in Kent a few years later, he began a diary largely devoted to natural history observations when he was only about thirteen. One of the earliest published entries, written shortly before his fifteenth birthday, describes a visit to the shore near the lighthouse at Crow Point, although he does not refer to it by name (throughout the *Journal* places and people are identified by their initial letters only – S for Saunton, V for Venn, I for Ilfracombe and so on). Wading up the estuary he suddenly sank to his waist in a sandpit. 'Knocked up my friend P— who is skipper of the ship N—, and asked if he had a fire so that I could dry myself. He replied that they had no fire but that his "missus" would look out a pair of pants for me'. These turned out to be a baggy pair of seaman's serge trousers in which the youthful diarist cycled home.

His friend was Charles Petherick, who with his wife Hester took care of the hospital ship *Nymphen,* bought by the Barnstaple Port Health Authority in 1892 for £275. Three years earlier a complaint had been made to the Collector of Customs at Bristol after a ship from Bahia in the East Indies had arrived at Appledore flying the yellow fever flag; the provision of *Nymphen* as what was called an Infectious Diseases Hospital for Seamen, at considerable expense, was the eventual result. No fewer than five wards were constructed – and in the 35 years she lay at permanent anchor on the mud near the lighthouse, she received just one patient.

Henry Williamson knew *Nymphen* well, and wrote of her in his novel *The Pathway,* published in 1928. However, the caretaker he attributed to her – an ex-whaler who had suffered so severely from frost-bite that he had lost his ears and an arm, and become deaf and dumb – had nothing in common with Charles Petherick. Willie Maddison and Mary Ogilvie, walking along the shore near Crow Point, saw 'the black mass of the beached hospital ship looming bigger and blacker as they approached it. The hull was shored upright with props, and held by chains stretched over their heads and secured to rusty anchors halfburied in the low sandy cliff'. Mary remarks that it is going to be sold – as indeed *Nymphen* was in 1927 – and Willie at once has the idea that they might buy it and live in it. His death, not long afterwards, puts paid to this romantic idea.Note 7

Williamson had known and loved the Burrows since his first enraptured fortnight spent on holiday in Georgeham in May, 1914. No one has captured their essential spirit as he did, not only in *The Pathway* but in other books.

During the eight years of his first period of life in Georgeham, 1921 to 1929, he valued his friendship with Dr Frederick Elliston Wright, who in his spare time made an exhaustive study of all aspects of the natural history of the area. 'He was an expert, a scientific naturalist; he knew all the wild flowers, the rare rushes and ferns, of the Saunton Burrows . . . we had often roamed there together, he the master, I the mere sensuous writer'. When Dr Wright's *Braunton: A Few Nature*

Notes appeared in 1926, Williamson reviewed it in the *North Devon Journal* and reproduced the review in the 'Books and Authors' section of *The Linhay on the Downs*. Whenever he could, he recommended the book to anyone likely to be interested.

The subtitle is 'A Few Nature Notes, with Lists of Flora, Macro Lepidoptera and Birds known to occur in the District'. The first edition contained some fifty drawings by the author, but the second, brought out in 1932, had many more, as well as several photographs, one of them showing Dr Wright, thin-stemmed pipe in mouth, holding a baby Barn Owl. He recorded that 'The Barn, the Tawny, and Little Owls are common here. The Long Eared Owl is plentiful, the Short Eared Owl comes in numbers as an autumn migrant; they occasionally stay and nest in the Burrows. I have also seen them nesting in the Marshes'. Henry Williamson, who by the time of his arrival to live in Skirr Cottage in 1921 had adopted the Barn Owl as his personal totem, would have found his friend's studies of these birds of particular interest.

Dr Wright (1879-1966) qualified in 1904, and served for a while as an opthalmic surgeon at St. Thomas's Hospital, but by 1906 had left London to join a Braunton practice. In the 1920s he was the senior partner, and a well-known local character. With an aged trilby crushed down over his cars, he rode a motorbike on most journeys, medical and otherwise, although in his young days he liked to ride a pony, his feet dangling because he disdained stirrups. At one time he was the part-owner of *Agnes,* a west country sailing ketch, which traded round the coast. (This vessel, built in Bude in 1835, had been rebuilt in 1904.) Occasionally the fancy took him to go for a voyage in her, with her captain, Will Mitchell. He liked to visit Lundy, and contributed three articles to the 'Journal of the Botanical Society' on its flora. A plant that is said to grow on the island and nowhere else bears his name: formerly classified as *Brassicella Wrightii,* it is now known as *Rynchosinopsis Wrightii.* His obituary was written for the Transactions of the Devonshire Association by Professor Leslie Harvey, Head of Zoology at Exeter University, who observed that he had 'made the Burrows his own, so much so that his little book *Braunton: A Few Nature Notes* still remains a mine of information . . . He knew the plants, birds, beetles, butterflies and moths particularly, but, like the good field man he was, nothing escaped his attention'.

He did not confine his interest to the Burrows, however. Visiting

Halsinger Bog in 'the most beautiful valley in the district' he found Sundew and Ivy leaved Bell Flower, Lesser Skullcap, Marsh Violet, Heath Bent Grass, Bog Asphodel and many other plants, including 'Sphagnum Moss forming large bosses in dry weather of yellowish white tinged with green'. At Spreacombe he explored the old mine workings. In 'the interior of the mine entrance, the floor and rocky sides gleam in places with sheets of bright golden green light, which are due to Luminous Moss (*Schistostega Osmundacea*)'. At first he supposed that the light was caused by phosphorescence, but later realized that it was due to reflection from special cells 'in a way similar to the reflection of light from the tapetum of cats' eyes at night'.

He may not have viewed with much enthusiasm the building of a number of timber chalets in the northern end of the dunes during the interwar years, which made it possible for people to spend holidays there and, conceivably, disturb wild life. A line of beach huts also appeared, though these were for day use only. There were surfers, even then; long before the days of wet suits, they simply lay flat on plywood boards to coast in under the high breakers.

Small aircraft flew over, circling the bay or heading for Lundy with mail, stores or passengers. The somewhat grandiosely named Barnstaple, or Barnstaple and North Devon Aerodrome or Airport, was formally opened in June, 1934, on 45 acres of the former Chivenor Farm, leased from Sir William Williams of Heanton. A few years later there were rumours that Braunton's remarkable survival of medieval strip farming, the Great Field, might be taken over by the Air Ministry for use as an RAF station, but in the event the Barnstaple Aerodrome and the adjoining Marsh Farm were chosen. RAF Chivenor opened as a Coastal Command training station in October, 1940.

After the outbreak of the Second World War, large areas of the Burrows were mined and in 1943 they and the beach became a training ground for United States assault troops preparing for D Day. Tank landing craft and amphibious vehicles ground to and fro, inevitably destroying the marram grass that bound the dunes. Part of the ancient ferry road was resurfaced, and is still known as the American Road.

The clearing of mines after 1945 was a slow business; for a number of years there were occasional explosions, sometimes because an unfortunate dog, running among the sandhills, triggered a forgotten mine.

In April, 1951, under the headline 'War Office want 1,500 Acres', it was reported in the *North Devon Journal-Herald* (as it was then) that a large part of the Burrows and Saunton beach, the whole of the area around Crow Point and the greater part of Instow beach were being requested as an infantry training ground, where live ammunition might be fired. An enquiry was held in Barnstaple's Guildhall the following month. Dr Wright represented the Botanical Society and other natural history organisations and, in Professor Harvey's words 'played a prominent part and acted a star role in the witness box with striking effect. That the southern half was saved to become a National Nature Reserve, while some of the worst effects of the middle area were ameliorated, can be attributed in large measure to his intervention'.

Yet the result of the enquiry was that the army was able to lease from John Christie, the owner of Tapeley Court and of the whole dune system, virtually everything they had asked for, while offering assurances that damage to terrain and wildlife would be avoided as far as possible. In December, 1960, the whole question of the use of the Burrows by what was still known as the War Department was discussed again. For some reason the press and, presumably, the public were excluded this time, but it was later announced that a new agreement had been reached for the continued use of 902 acres of the Burrows and nearly 400 acres of the foreshore as a combined operations training area in which the firing of small arms, mortars and demolition charges of up to 100 pounds would be permitted. The army authorities arranged that public access to the area would be restricted to no more than thirty days a year.

In April, 1964, the Nature Conservancy Council (now English Nature) signed a lease with the War Department for about 560 acres of duneland at Crow Point, and another 932 acres of the Burrows, to constitute a reserve which would be open whenever they were not being used for military exercises. A warden was appointed, and plans were made to begin work to check erosion; much replanting of marram grass had to be carried out to heal the ravaged dunes.

Pairs of noticeboards in the car parks at Sandy Lane and Broad Sands and at several points between them where paths branch from the American Road into the Burrows, offer an ironic contrast. Those

set up by English Nature welcome visitors to the Reserve, and tell them something of the plants and wild creatures they expect may to find there, but alongside each one is a red MOD board, warning that no one is to pass it if red flags are flying – without indicating that the nearest is to be looked for on a flagpole that surmounts a high dune some distance west of the Sandy Lane car park, not visible from many parts of the Burrows. It seems possible that some nervous visitors may be deterred from venturing any further even when no red flags are flying, especially if they have consulted Ordnance maps which bear the words 'Danger Area' across a large central section of the Burrows, on a stretch of the foreshore and east of Crow Point. However it does not seem that the red flag flies often, and military exercises, when they happen, tend to be on the estuary shore. On most days of the year anyone can wander freely over this range of miniature mountains formed by the wind and fixed by plants.

Whatever surface American troops laid down on the old ferry road in 1943 has long gone. A series of deep scrapes and potholes runs for well over a mile south from Sandy Lane car park. In wet weather they turn to puddles and ponds, sometimes several yards long and the full width of the road – which is probably left unrepaired to deter motorists, who can reach Broad Sands and Crow Point by the Toll Road from Velator.

Thickets of willow and hawthorn border the rough road, with an undergrowth of bramble. Big patches of privet grow here and there; it seems strange to encounter this characteristic shrub of the suburban gardens in such a place. Moving westwards away from the road one comes to the first and highest of the three ridges of dunes that form the Burrows. Level areas between them are called slacks, some dry and firm underfoot except after heavy rain, others usually wet. Each of these has been given a name, several harking back to the war: Shooting Butts Slack, Bomber Slack, Shrapnel Slack and DUKW Slack. Others are more peaceful: Bee Slack, Partridge Slack and Five Ponds Slack. A profile of the dunes provided by the Nature Conservancy's boards shows three smooth billows – dune pasture, dune ridge, slack, dune ridge, slack, foredune and beach – but any sense of this tidy diagram is lost in the wonderfully complex and irregular reality of hummock and hollow, rough scrub and smooth sand slopes, turf and marram grass.

Thousands of snails live – and die – on the Burrows; their faded

empty shells are scattered widely. Naturalists say that many die of sunstroke if the temperature rises above a certain point, which makes it strange that they choose a habitat where the sand can grow burningly hot on sunny days in summer. Holes in sandy banks, and scrapes in turf and innumerable droppings, show rabbits have recovered to some extent from the man-made plague of myxamytoses that first attacked them in 1954. Yet there is now a new threat to them, viral haemorrhagic disease – and without rabbit grazing, long grass and bushy thickets quickly take over, smothering the flowering carpet. English Nature have introduced Soay sheep, initially on 42 acres, to help control unwanted vegetation.

More than 400 species of flowering plant are said to grow here. As a serious botanist, Dr Wright listed them at the end of his, using their Latin names only. He also included all the ferns, rushes, sedges and grasses he had identified, both on the Burrows and on the Marsh, which he called the Mares (Barbellion's Mires). In his all-too short botanical chapters he mentions just a few of them by their English names, adding the Latin ones in brackets. The wanderer on the dunes may still come upon them today: in the spring a profusion of the lovely little yellow pansy which he called *Viola Curtisii*, rare elsewhere; wild orchids – the Pyramidal, Early Purple and Southern Marsh; in summer, Viper's Bugloss, Restharrow, Marsh Helleborine, Yellow Bartsia, Centaury, Sea Holly, Yellow Horned Poppy and, towards the Saunton end, the Great Sea Stock. Dr Wright was doubtful about the Stock's chances of survival, and thought that it should be protected. but, seventy years after he was writing, in spite of so much military activity during the war and since, it is still to be seen. The most conspicuous flower of summer, apart from the ubiquitous Ragwort, is the Evening Primrose. Underfoot are Thyme, Eyebright, big patches of Haresfoot Clover and of mosses as bronze in autumn as those Tomlinson saw near the remains of St. Anne's Chapel in 1917. In dry slacks the 'crisp grey lichen' which Dr Wright identified as Reindeer Moss crunches underfoot.

Dwarf willow creeps over the ground; from a distance, in early summer, its seeding flowerheads give the impression of white flowers. Towards Saunton, big clumps of alder, no more than four or five feet high, are apparently not a dwarf species, but are stunted by the strong Atlantic winds that have heaped up the dunes and shape and reshape them constantly, like a sculptor never satisfied with his work.

The Burrows: a tiny fragment of an overcrowded island. Just four miles long and about a mile and a half wide, they are vulnerable to any kind of human disturbance. By an accident of geography they have existed, since the beginning of the Second World War, as a constant witness to warlike activities – not only army exercises on the ground but, except for a period of six years when RAF Chivenor was closed, the almost daily roar of aircraft. The station closed again on 17th March, 1995. The Ministry of Defence is said to be considering moving Royal Marine Logistics Units to the base. That the Nature Reserve has been designated a Biosphere Reserve of international importance may offer some protection; possibly it will ensure that, if any increased use is proposed, the area will have many champions as resolute and knowledgeable as that devoted lover of the Dunes, Dr Frederick Elliston Wright.

14

View from High Ground

The highest point of the long ridge of Saunton Down is 518 feet above sea level – or 158 metres according to modern maps. It can be reached by climbing the ancient main road from South Hole to the estuary, which has been given two names: Hole Lane on its northern side and Hannaborough Lane on its southern. It goes up steeply on either side, muddy in some places in wet weather, worn to the bedrock in others. To the west of Saunton Court two waymarked paths wind over the saddle of the Down to join a lane leading down to Croyde village.

Walking westwards along the ridge, it is possible to see almost the whole of the north-west corner of Devon, as though from a low-flying aircraft. Immediately below the northern slope lie South and North Hole, held as a single manor by the Saxon Etmar before he was dispossessed in 1066. Farther away one can see parts of Georgeham and Croyde, with Pickwell set back between them and Morte Point barring the distance to the west. Southwards, the olive-green hinterland of Saunton beach stretches for more than a mile inland over Braunton Great Field and Braunton Marsh. The hills and hollows of the dunes appear strangely flattened from this height. On their seaward side, the tawny sands end at the silvery glitter of the estuary, and line after line of white breakers unfold and slide into the shallows.

On clear days, the long coastline running down to Hartland can be seen, and Lundy, a dark bar on the horizon – but often sea-mist or sun-haze hide them.

Looking out to the Great Field, one is seeing a remnant of an agricultural landscape probably established by some of the first Saxons to settle in this part of Devon. It has been suggested that the Great Field may have been carved out at the end of the 7th century. Originally part of a much larger area of strip cultivation running northwards across what has become the built-up area of Braunton, it is now restricted to about 350 acres; where there were some 500 strips in the mid-19th century, there are today only a fraction of that number. They are grouped into larger fields with names that echo back to medieval times – Pitlands, Cutabarrow, Hayditch, Longhedgelands, Lower, Middle and Higher Thorn and Gallowell.

Strips were about a furlong – 220 yards – long, and a chain, or 22 yards, wide. This area of 4840 square yards established the land measurement of the acre, formally recognised by Edward I in 1305. 'It was based on the amount of land which a man with two oxen could plough in a day – 40 rods long by 4 rods wide. The rod, which was a pole used to drive the oxen, was 5½ yards long.[Note 1] The little river Caen borders the Great Field on its eastern side, its name a legacy of the Normans who took over the rich manor of Braunton on behalf of the Conqueror.[Note 2]

To the south lies Braunton Marsh, a development belonging, not to the middle ages, but to the enthusiasm for land reclamation of the early 19th century. At a time when the Napoleonic Wars were still dragging on, a group of local landowners and farmers, including lords of the various manors – Braunton Arundel, Braunton Abbotts and Saunton – who had grazing rights on what were then tidal saltmarshes, got together and proposed to build a strong embankment to keep out the Taw. An act of Parliament was passed in 1811 to enable the work to begin. The massive embankment, running from Velator towards what was then still known as the Ferry House, was planned to protect a thousand acres. To walk the path along its broad spine (helpfully the stone walls that cross it at intervals are provided with steps) is to gain some idea of the tremendous labour involved, at a time when energy meant the muscle power of men and horses. The top of the bank is ten or twelve feet above the asphalted Toll Road that runs on its north side. The drainage channel, or delph, beyond

111

the road provided much of the material, although beach boulders and stone from the quarry on Saunton Down was added, and the surface was covered with puddled clay.

There can have been no unemployed working men in this part of north Devon during the years the river wall was being built; in fact local labour was not enough, and men were brought from Cornwall and Ireland, and even from Holland. The Dutch, with their knowledge of dyke building, were particularly useful; some of them supervised the construction of drainage ditches and sluices. The first part of the enterprise took four years, being completed in 1815, the year of Waterloo. In the mid-19th century, on the initiative of Frederick Williams of Heanton, a great deal more work was carried out; the quay at Velator was built and Braunton Pill was straightened so that small ships could sail up more easily. In June, 1857, the final gap was closed. According to a report in the 'North Devon Journal', work started at three o'clock on the morning of the 15th (so near midsummer, it would have begun to get light by then). About 250 men, using 130 carts – some of them lent by local farmers eager to see the job finished – started work at low tide. They had constructed what were described as barrow roads and a tramway. After about three hours steady work 'it became evident that old Neptune had been beaten on a portion of his own domain . . . Before evening the embankment was raised full six feet above the top water of the neap tide, and Horsey Island and Broadlands became permanently, it is hoped, united to the mainland, thus reclaiming a further 200 acres from the wash of the tide'. Dozens of onlookers cheered and drank the health of Frederick Williams, who congratulated the workmen on their achievement.

The Marsh, grazed by cattle and sheep in summer, is dotted with barns, many of them disused and roofless. The unusual circular linhay a short distance west of the Toll House was repaired and rethatched in the mid-1980s, but gales have torn the thatch away again. In May, flag iris outline drainage channels beside a long stretch of the Marsh Road in yellow, and everywhere, from spring to autumn, are flowering plants: rushes, sedges, tall graceful grasses, horsetails and the Great Reed Mace, usually known as the bulrush, bearing its chocolate-brown cylinders as the year passes.

Below the north-west end of Saunton Down lies Croyde beach and its narrow belt of dunes. Behind them is what was once always known as the Nalgo camp. In the 1930s the National Association of Local Government Officers bought the land to establish a holiday camp for its members. Every year, until the beginning of the Second World War, the arrival of 'they campers' was resented by many people in the two valley villages. More lucrative visitors, prepared to pay a few guineas for accommodation, were preferred, if there had to be strangers at all. The campers tended to be noisy and high-spirited and brightly dressed, and their North Country or Midland or London accents contrasted sharply with the slower Devon speech. They took up most of the beach near their camp and were good customers for the tea and ice cream huts that came into being. Up and down the sandhills children climbed and rolled, dogs ran; energetic games were played on the beach, deck chairs and surfboards were for hire, and new car parks opened. The campers brought increased custom to shops and pubs, yet were not always welcome. Charlie Ovey, of the Kings Arms in Georgeham, removed the skittle table from the bar in early summer, remarking that he 'couldn't abide to see it fooled about wi', and they campers playin' wild'. Although it was nothing to what would come a few decades later, the camp was the first sizeable development of tourism in the area.

A number of houses were built along the roads at either end of Croyde Bay in the years before and after the First World War. Since the 1950s a tide of suburbia has been allowed to sweep over large parts of north Devon, and Croyde has a conspicuous share. On the north side, a large caravan park fills fields that used to be farmland. But just beyond, a car park bears a familiar oakleaf symbol; 251 acres of the headland of Baggy were given to the National Trust in 1939. The donors were the Misses Connie and Florence Hyde, who lived at Croyde Bay House with their brother Edwin. Both Connie and Edwin appear to have been reclusive and invalidish, but Florence was active in the life of Georgeham parish, something of a local benefactress to causes and people of whom she approved, and also something of a busybody. (She is depicted as Miss Virginia Goff in Henry Williamson's novel *The Pathway,* and as Lady Maude Seeke in *Life in a Devon Village* and *Tales of a Devon Village:* her puritanical view of his behaviour during his early years in Georgeham had earned his resentment.) She was an enthusiastic gardener; she beautified Georgeham churchyard. The gift of Baggy, which had been bought by an uncle some fifty years earlier, was probably made on her initiative,

113

and remains an invaluable expression of her love for the place where she lived.

On beaches on either side of Baggy, in the days when lime was the principal agricultural fertilizer, limekilns were built. Little coasting ketches brought limestone from Wales, and the culm to burn it; they were beached to unload their cargoes between tides. Like others around the coast – including one at Woolacombe – the kilns had been abandoned by the end of the 19th century. In the early 1920s, the kiln at Croyde was taken over as a kitchen and storeroom by two sisters who sold ice cream, cold drinks and trays of tea (the kettles boiled on primus stoves) to visitors on the beach. (Today its beehiveshaped chambers, built into a bank for top filling, stand empty, useful as a shelter in sudden summer showers.) The cottages beside the kiln at Vention were converted into a single dwelling, at first on a modest scale, although later owners altered and enlarged it considerably. At about the same time someone built a shack of wood and asbestos sheeting at the top of the lane to Putsborough beach, and advertised it as a hotel, so successfully that two years later he was able to put up a more permanent building, which flourished for many years until it was converted to holiday flats in the 1980s. A large, ugly red building, Heathercombe Hotel, was put up on the side of Woolacombe Down in the late 1930s; it burned down during the war, and was not rebuilt.

Climbing the lane from Putsborough one day in April, 1930, Henry Williamson saw noticeboards announcing that it had been proposed to cut a road from Woolacombe to Croyde: 'here a great new coach road along the Severn sea is to work its way, levelling hedges, razing the grey rock which the lichens have known through all the centuries. . .' Note 3

To the relief of all who loved the bay, the project was abandoned after only about a mile of the stone-metalled roadway had been built across the side of Woolacombe Down. Now, on summer days, cars park along its whole length, facing the sea.

15

Old Village, New Resort

When the Norman lord, William Capra, or Chievre, was granted Woolacombe, in place of the Saxon Edwin, it was a fair-sized manor, worth £13.15s, a great deal more than any other – excluding Braunton – in the north-west corner of Devon, partly, perhaps, because it was grazed by no fewer than 300 sheep. By contrast the manor of Mortehoe was small. Its Saxon lord, Edric, was displaced by Ralph de Limisei, a nephew of William the Conqueror. Paying geld on only half a hide, or about sixty acres, it was worth a mere ten shillings a year, and was worked by two villeins and a serf. However, over the centuries it grew into a large parish of over four thousand acres, taking in Ossaborough, Shaftesborough and Eastacott, as well as Woolacombe – much as the small settlement of Georgeham grew to include Norman manors previously of greater importance.

It seems impossible to know when Mortehoe's church of St. Mary Magdalene was built, or by whom. 'The oldest part of the church is the tower on the north side connected to the church by a low round-headed doorway. The tower is unbuttressed and unpinnacled. The north door, presumably the entry into a north porch, is pointed and rudely built of large stones'.[Note 1] The first known reference to a church at Mortehoe occurs in the registers of Bishop Walter Stapledon of Exeter, recording that in 1308 the then rector, Sir William de

Tracy, founded a chantry dedicated to Saints Mary and Catherine. (Before 1384, incumbents of Mortehoe were rectors; after that date, the church was appropriated to the Dean and Chapter of Exeter, and the parish became a vicarage.) The existence of a church before 1308 is implied by the fact that Tracy had two predecessors: John Allesworthy, 1258-1275, and a priest known only as Sir Thomas, 1275-1307.

William de Tracy died in 1322. His imposing tomb chest, nearly seven feet long, is in the transept, and for several centuries has been the object of controversy. In appearance, it is certainly a remarkable and mysterious sepulchre. Around the sides are panels of some kind of sandstone, worn by time; damage has been patched in a number of places with newer stone. At the head is a crudely-rendered crucifixion; at the sides are two indistinct figures said to represent Saints Mary and Catherine, and tracery showing two and three-light blank arches, quatrefoils and circles. The foot is blank, and much repaired. A large crack may be seen on the south side, near the head. Despite their condition, the panels give the impression of being less ancient than the massive slab, some seven inches thick, that lies upon the tomb. Of an entirely different stone, it has been described as granite, which it clearly is not, and as black marble. Lead-grey, it resembles the dense type of slate seen in some parts of North Wales. Incised on it is a roughly depicted figure of a priest in full vestments, holding a chalice. The hardly decipherable inscription, in Norman French and Lombardic characters, is said to read 'Syre . . . ame de Trac . . . Alme eyt Mercy', originally 'Sir William de Tracy, may God have mercy on his soul'.

The first person to suggest, in print, that this William de Tracy was the knight of the same name who took part in the murder of Thomas à Becket in Canterbury Cathedral in 1170, seems to have been William Camden. Camden is said to have made a journey to Ilfracombe in 1588 when he was gathering material for a second edition of his *Magna Britannica,* and to have been made Prebendary of Ilfracombe the following year. (Since Camden was, and remained, a layman, this presentation appears as an example of the remarkable way in which benefices might be distributed, in those days, as a mark of personal favour.) *The Dictionary of National Biography* observes that 'According to tradition Camden resided in the ancient vicarage, which he in part rebuilt. After a more extensive reconstruction c.1759, his coat of arms remained to be seen in a room that had been turned into a kitchen until 1888'. It may be assumed that during his first visit to Ilfracombe, Camden went to look at Mortehoe church – probably having been told of the Tracy tomb – and jumped to the wrong conclusion. Camden claimed that Tracy had retired to Mortehoe thirteen years after the murder of Becket, adding loftily 'contrary to what the vulgar chroniclers say, that all who were concerned in that murder died miserably in three years after'.

Risdon, writing about fifty years after Camden, repeated his story almost word for word, and Westcote, who had met Camden, also gave it currency. However, to turn to the *Dictionary of National Biography* again, the entry concerning the murderous Tracy points out that 'there were evidently living at this period two men who bore the name, and it is impossible to distinguish with certainty between them, or to decide which of them is to be identified as the subject of this article'. The writer draws on the work of a contemporary, who collected 'Materials for a History of Becket'. According to this, Tracy went to confess his guilt to his diocesan bishop, Bartholomew of Exeter. Afterwards he and his fellow assassins – Reginald FitzUrse, Hugh de Norville and Richard Brito – spent some time in Knaresborough and in Scotland. Tracy then travelled to Rome to surrender himself to the Pope's mercy. His penance was to make his way to the Holy Land to serve under the Knights Templars for fourteen years, spending his time praying and fasting; the last dated reference to him as a living man was in 1172, when he was at a papal court. 'The legends which tell either that Tracy never started on his pilgrimage at all, or that he returned secretly and lived for many years in some lonely spot on the Devonshire coast, are baseless'. On his journey towards the Holy Land, Tracy got no further than southern Italy. At Cosenza, in Calabria, he was 'smitten with a horrible disease, his flesh decaying while he was yet alive, so that he could not refrain from tearing it off with his own hands, and he died in agony, praying incessantly to St. Thomas'. (This sounds alarmingly like a medieval case of necrotising fascilitis, the disease that caused media panic in Britain in 1994, but it may simply have been gangrene.)

The Sir William de Tracy whose tomb gave rise to the legend was almost certainly a member of the Tracy family who were lords of the manor of Barnstaple from the mid-12th century, when Henry de Tracy, a descendant of the first Norman lord of the borough, Judhel de

Totnes, received it from King Stephen. Another Henry de Tracy, great-grandson of the first, built Barnstaple's first bridge in the later years of his life. He also founded a chapel on the bridge, dedicated to the canonized Becket, which indicates a wish to expiate a crime committed by a man who may have been a distant relation of an earlier generation. William, rector of Mortehoe, was a younger contemporary of the bridge-building Henry, who died in 1274 at the age of 77, as was Oliver de Tracy, rector of Georgeham from 1261 to 1272; it is not impossible that the latter was Henry's brother, and William was his son or grandson.

The Victorian fashion for restoring parish churches reached Mortehoe in 1857, when the Revd John Derby Ness, curate and later vicar of Mortehoe from 1826 to 1884, helped by some members of his family, paid for work to be done in memory of his eldest son. He sought the advice of R.D. Gould, the architect who for fifty years was Borough Surveyor of Barnstaple. As a result the singing gallery at the west end was taken out, the contents of graves under the floor reburied in the churchyard, old box pews with doors and numbered seats were removed, windows were enlarged and much clear glass was replaced by memorial windows. Some of the splendid carved bench ends, thought to date back to the 16th century, are said by Dr George Blundell Longstaff, People's Warden from 1878 to 1916, to have been renewed, and those at the west end bearing the initials of the vicar's family to have been added. The whole cost was some £1,200, of which Mr Ness paid £1,000. (Dr Longstaff, M.P., J.P., who lived at Twitchen, later commissioned the striking mosaic over the chancel arch, designed by Selwyn Image, in memory of his wife. It shows four Pre-Raphaelite style angels surmounted by a representation of the Lamb and Cross in a medallion, on a background of gilt tesserae.)

The most questionable and even macabre part of the 'restoration' was the opening of the Tracy tomb. It seems that the only eye-witness account of this is contained in some recollections written by a local inhabitant, Henry Watts, a builder by trade, who served as sexton for at least fifty years, and in 1886 helped to build the handsome lychgate to the churchyard. His manuscript, in 'laborious longhand' is in the possession of the church. He claimed – somewhat surprisingly, as he was only ten years old at the time – to have seen the open tomb and within it a headless skeleton and three huge nails with heads as big as

119

the halfpenny coins of those days. There was no lead coffin. It was known that the tomb had been broken into at some earlier time, and it has been said that the coffin was used as a pigs' trough on a neighbouring farm. According to Mr Watts, the skeleton was removed temporarily, and 'Mr Thomas Smith of Duckpool Farm, a big stout man, went and stretched himself out in the tomb out of curiosity'. He deduced that the occupant of the tomb had been a bigger man than he was – though whether he made allowance for the space once taken up by the coffin is not clear. The remains were replaced and the tomb closed again. Much of the damage to the panels, and some of the consequent patching with plain sandstone, is presumably attributable to this piece of ecclesiastical vandalism. The absence of a skull, if Mr Watts' childhood memories are reliable, adds a chilling final touch to the enigma of the tomb.

It was decreed, by an Order in Council of 1896, that no more burials were to be permitted in the small graveyard of Mortehoe church after the following May. A new cemetery was opened some 200 yards west of the village, on a gentle slope overlooking the sea, a short distance from the entrance gateway to what is now the National Trust land of Morte Point.

In 1850, Mortehoe was described as 'a scattered village, five miles west of Ilfracombe, picturesquely situated on the sea coast, where that rocky promontory, called Morte Point, juts out more than a mile into the Bristol Channel, between Rockham and Morte Bays, where there is a dangerous reef of rocks, on which vessels have often been wrecked.'[Note 2]

Not only on Morte Point but on both sides of the headland, many small ships – schooners, barques, brigs and smacks – are known to have been wrecked in the 19th and early 20th centuries. The naturalist Philip Gosse, exploring the coast west of Ilfracombe in about 1851, remarked that five ships had been lost on Morte the previous year. It seems that not all these losses were due to bad weather or navigational error. Fifteen years before Mary Hartley published her verse description of the wreck of the *Meridian* near Saunton lighthouse, the Revd Charles C. Crump, rector of Halford, Warwickshire, had brought out a somewhat similar pamphlet, containing nearly 250 lines of doggedly rhymed couplets, dedicated to the President of the Shipwrecked Fishermen and Mariners' Benevolent Society. He called it 'The Morte Stone: a Tale of the Coast. Based on Facts', adding that

it was 'a remonstrance against the system of wrecking and an appeal for shipwrecked seamen'.

He began by describing the rescue of the crew of the *Thomas Crisp*, a merchant brig wrecked on Morte, from Rockham Bay by a steam vessel, the *Cornwall*. Then, having brought in the legend of the murderous Sir William de Tracy and his supposed years spent in remorseful retirement at Mortehoe, he accused the people of the village and neighbouring hamlets of being wreckers. Mixing his metaphors somewhat, he called them 'rabid wolves, the vampires of Morte Bay'. (By contrast, the Morte Bay farmers were 'ever prompt to succour the distressed'.) With energetic rhetoric he demanded to know what England was going to do about it, and foresaw that there would be a 'beacon light' that would 'point the way to safety through the night'.

As an appendix, he reproduced a 'Memorial presented to the Trinity Board, London, from North Devon, etc., on the subject of the Morte Stone' dated February, 1850. In this, 'Clergyman, Gentlemen, Shipowners, Merchants, Traders, and others, resident at Bideford, Appledore, Barnstaple, Mortehoe, Ilfracombe and places adjoining' drew attention to the fact that 'numerous disasters to Trading Vessels, with great loss of life, and of much valuable property, are of yearly occurrence'. They added that a good deal of the loss was due to 'the barbarous conduct of lawless wreckers from neighbouring hamlets'. A hopeful final note, dated from Ilfracombe in August, 1850, said that the Elder Brethren of Trinity House had 'signified their intention to . . . erect a Lighthouse at Morte, on condition of a toll, of one eighth of a penny per ton, to be paid by Merchant Vessels passing the Lighthouse'.

For whatever reason (was the toll plan unworkable?) it was another 29 years before a 55-foot tower was built on a rocky platform below the top of the cliff at Bull Point (which many people considered was the wrong site) at a cost of about £7,000. It had a fixed red light to warn shipping of the position of the Morte Stone, and a powerful foghorn.

During the three decades before the lighthouse was built some ten ships were wrecked on the stretch of coast from Morte Point to Bull Point. The RNLI decided to station a lifeboat at Woolacombe in 1871 as a subsidiary to the Ilfracombe boat; she was the *Grace Woodbury*, formerly the *Jack-a-Jack*. However, because to the difficulties of launching her – and her successor – from the beach, using horses, as at Saunton, she only went out on rescue twice in 29 years, and was withdrawn at the end of that time.**Note 3** The existence of a Rocket Apparatus team from 1890 was of considerably greater use in saving lives.

When the railway line was extended from Barnstaple to Ilfracombe in 1874, Mortehoe acquired a station. Almost at once, a few people began to offer accommodation for visitors. (The post office seems to have operated as an unofficial tourist information centre: it announced 'Local information afforded to visitors on application'.) By 1878 there were three lodging house keepers: William Whately at Duke's Cottage, Samuel Conibear at Barricane House and Richard Gammon at Rockley House (the latter was a grocer; he also owned and presumably hired out carriages). Henry Watts, the builder/sexton, offered accommodation at Victoria House, which he may well have built for himself. There were three public houses: the New Inn and two named in tribute to the principal landowners, the Fortescue Arms and the Chichester Arms. The village had two blacksmiths (Samuel Conibear was one of them), two carpenters, two bakers, a shopkeeper who probably kept a general store, and a boot and shoemaker. There were also five builders, a remarkable number for so small a village – but they may have known that their services would soon be much in demand.

In the late 1870s Woolacombe (often spelled Wollacombe, as in earlier centuries) was still only a tiny hamlet of half a dozen cottages. The manor mill, its big overshot waterwheel powered by a stream running down the valley, stood on the 800-acre Barton Farm, the property of Sir Bruce Chichester of Arlington. (His father, John Palmer Chichester, known as Arlington Jack, had served in the navy and represented Barnstaple in parliament from 1831 to 1841: in 1840 he had been created a baronet as 'a tribute to his constant support of Liberal principles'.)

Within a few years everything changed. A developer, an architect and surveyor from Barnstaple named Arnold Thorne, saw the attraction of the sands of what was still known as Morte Bay rather than Woolacombe Bay. He bought land and began to build. The Woolacombe Bay Hotel arose, bold in red brick, and was so successful that it had to be enlarged in 1897 to accommodate 150 guests. By 1889 Woolacombe was described as a favourite seaside resort. Nos 1, 2, 3 and 4 Seymour Villas, No. 1 Fortescue Villas, No. 1 Rockham Villas and No.2 Marine Villas were all lodging houses. A Mrs Smith owned no fewer than three guest houses: Gordon Lodge, Thorn Lodge and Lundy House. Richard Gammon had evidently prospered: a firm named Gammon and Son were not only grocers, dairymen, general dealers and livery stable owners and postmasters, but ran a private boarding house and lodging house.[Note 4]

During the next decade the term 'lodging house' had apparently fallen out of favour; people now stayed in apartments. These were available at most of the houses previously listed, and at some new ones, but the most imposing seems to have been the 'Avondale Boarding Establishment and Private Apartments, commanding extensive views of Woolacombe Bay and sands. Hot and cold baths; every home comfort under personal supervision; good accommodation for cyclists; close to golf links; terms moderate. Mrs Mary Petherham, proprietoress'.[Note 5]

The arrival of an estate agent suggests that properties had begun to change hands fairly frequently. The Barnstaple-born philanthropist, William Rock, had built and endowed a Convalescent Home in 1888, and a Revd Thomas of Bristol had founded a Seaside Home for Ministers and their wives.

Residents of this new, growing Woolacombe evidently tired of climbing the steep hill to Mortehoe church; in 1841 a small structure of corrugated iron was put up as a place of worship. By the end of the Edwardian era this was replaced by a church of red sandstone dedicated to St. Sabinus, one of the Irish holy men who are said to have crossed the Bristol Channel in search of converts.

Although Woolacombe was a small resort, in comparison with many on the south coast of Devon, its appearance displeased some visitors. A writer in 1908 lamented that 'The long, steep road that descends from Mortehoe to the flat shore of Woolacombe Bay, is becoming plagued with a growth of tasteless lodging houses, where neutral-tinted stucco is put to shame by the splendour of sea, sky and sands. . . refreshment caterers have descended upon the place with tents . . . The safe bathing in the sea, and the extensive golfing in the sandhills or in the flat fields have converted what was, literally, a "howling waste" – for the winds occasionally blow great guns here – into the semblance of a seaside resort. There were, but a few years ago, only some three houses here, including the old manor mill,

whose waterwheel formed a picturesque object beside the little stream that empties itself into the bay; but now there is a great red brick hotel with the usual "special terms to golfers", and a little red town has sprung up around it, with a fringe of rather blear-eyed shops facing the sea, and some better, turned at right angles to it. There is so impossible a look about the whole thing . . . it looks, with its refreshment booths and array of chairs on the shore in summer, like some camp meeting in a desolate part of America. . . Only a fanatical golfer, to whom the world beyond his putting-greens and his bunkers is merely incidental, could long find occupation here.[Note 6]

Originally of only nine holes, the golf course was extended to eighteen in 1910; it covered eighty acres, and stretched for about a mile along Woolacombe Warren. The annual subscription in Edwardian days was 31s 6d., or visitors could pay 7s 0d per week. A guide book of 1905 called it a very sporting course: 'The hazards are all natural, formidable sandhills, some sixty feet in height, loose sand bunkers, a road with open ditch, and other obstacles. The greens are well maintained and the lies are good'[Note 7] (The coming of war in 1939 put an end to this course, and the Warren, the property of the National Trust, is once more an open space.)

In 1908 the Great Western was running a service from Paddington that included a 10.30 a.m. train that reached Ilfracombe at 4.26 and an 11.50 that arrived at 5.08. The London and South Western's fast trains left Waterloo at 11.10 a.m. and 12 noon, and reached Ilfracombe at 4.23 and 5.28 respectively. These trains would have stopped at Mortehoe station, and holiday-makers arriving to stay in either Mortehoe or Woolacombe would have been able to hire carriages to their boarding houses or apartments. It can hardly be imagined that as they drove down the last long hill into Woolacombe, and saw the wide bay opening ahead of them, they supposed themselves to be arriving at a place that could be called desolate or impossible.

Until after the Second World War, building went on comparatively slowly, but now the roads from both Mortehoe village and Mortehoe station are lined with houses, bungalows and small hotels, and caravan and camping sites fill many fields to the north and east. Pevsner, in 1988, was sharply critical: 'along the seafront a fringe of Victorian and Edwardian villas; behind them a formless spread of 20th century seaside flats, an insult to the glorious sweep of the bay'.

Yet it might have been much worse. The whole of the hinterland of

126

the bay, and perhaps parts of its sheltering headlands, might have been covered with houses, shops and their service roads. That this did not happen is largely due to a few individuals. The headlands were protected first. Thirty years before the Misses Hyde gave Baggy, Miss Rosalie Chichester of Arlington, only child of Sir Bruce, began a series of gifts to the National Trust: Morte Point in 1920 in memory of her parents, Potter's Hill in 1936 to celebrate George V's Silver Jubilee, and later Woolacombe Warren, the former golf course. It is interesting that these benefactors happened to be women of property who, having no need to consider the wishes of husbands and children, made it possible for innumerable people of all ages to enjoy these places for the foreseeable future.

16

At the Far Headland

Morte Point and Baggy Point are in many ways dissimilar. Baggy is longer, wider and generally higher, a gently undulating, steep-sided tableland sometimes rising to over 300 feet above sea level; it has a fairly good depth of soil and, except at the far western end, is cultivated. Its underlying rock is sandstone of the Devonian period. Devon has the distinction among English counties of giving its name to a whole period of geological time, the immensely ancient Upper Palaeolithic, between about 395 and 345 million years ago. Devonian rocks – shales, sandstones, limestones and slates, deposited in shallow sea – create the landscape of North Devon. Geological maps of an area stretching across to West Somerset neaten the complexity of what lies under the earth; they show a series of more or less parallel bands lying between the Bristol Channel coast and the Taw, each one named from a locality – Lynton Beds, Ilfracombe Beds, Pickwell Down Beds and so on. Baggy gives its name to one of these, Mortehoe to another. Mortehoe Beds are slate. On the headland the rock, split and striated and white veined in places with quartz, tapers westwards to just above the sea. It shows gradations of colour from anthracite grey at the tideline to silver-green on the higher slopes. Flat seaworn pebbles in tiny inlets only a few feet wide are pale in sunlight. At the tip of the headland is the palest rock of all, soapy-smooth to the touch, a remarkable contrast to the hard sandstone of Baggy, and deeply pitted in places as though huge fingers had pushed into dough.

Offshore, the Morte Stone is jagged and dark. Lieut. Denham, writing 'Sailing Directions for Lundy and the North Coast of Devon' in 1832, remarked that 'in the Sandy Bay of Morte' vessels might 'hover in settled weather, to cheat either flood or ebb under weigh; or drop an anchor in six or seven fathoms, on clear bottom anywhere, within the points, at half a mile offshore.'Note 1

A rocky ledge is said to extend for 3½ cables, or more than a mile, westwards from the point, 'and near the centre of this ledge is Morte Stone, only covered for a short time at high water springs.' An ebb tide 'sits clear of the Stone, but flood or North-East going stream, across Morte Bay, sits directly over the ledge; there is, besides, a dangerous race off the point in bad weather which must be avoided . . . When rounding Morte Stone during thick weather, a vessel should keep in depths of not less than 20 fathoms.'

So, half a mile off shore, the water is from 36 to 42 feet deep, and further out is at least 120 feet deep. Yet in the time when sea levels are said to have been much lower than they are today – seven, nine, ten thousand years ago – the small groups of people who lived in this part of Devon would have been able to walk out towards Lundy on dry land. The patient, scholarly guesswork that is the archaeology of that period, surmising a whole way of life from fragments of stone, bone and pottery, can offer only a faint picture of their lives. It was colder then, as the climate began slowly to warm after the last Ice Age. It seems significant that it is on the southern slopes of Morte, Baggy and Saunton Down that collections of their worked flints have been found: probably they were making the most of the sun's warmth. Yet why did they work on high ground, when lower levels would surely have offered better shelter?

Morte is formed of a series of tors, with turfy hollows between them. On the crests of some, outcrops of rock stick up like the discoloured teeth of giants. The slate's bone has only a thin skin of poor soil on which gorse and bracken grow, and a few patches of heather, but it seems unlikely that any arable crop, even oats, has ever flourished here. In the hollows sheep graze, although some of them make a goatlike way along the steeper slopes above the sea, and others lie in the shelter of outcrops, looking like boulders, and are not

alarmed by the familiar sight of wandering human beings.

Silvery lichen clings to silvery rock. There is thyme in the turf, seathrift, pink clover, some kind of small hawkbit and what looks like perennial centaury, despite the fact that it is said the be 'very rare in maritime turf in N. Cornwall and N. Pembrokeshire'. Possibly it's simply a dwarfed form of common centaury. Growing freely on walls in the town, a wild plant and a garden escape spread out together to brighten the cliffside with purple and gold: big shrubby clumps of common mallow and some very hardy member of the *senecio* family.

Morte: the farthest north-west of Devon. Seaward, out beyond Lundy, due west for more than two thousand miles, is Battle Harbour, on the coast of Labrador. To the north, only twenty miles across the Bristol Channel, is Worm's Head, the western point of the Gower, beloved of Dylan Thomas. Just a mile or so to the north-east is Bull Point; its lighthouse blinks weakly in the sunshine; it flashes constantly by day and night to indicate to shipping that it has become an automatic light.

After 93 years of regular operation, its continued existence was threatened by cliff erosion; in the early hours of 24th September, 1972, fifteen metres of cliff fell into the sea, and another fifteen metres subsided, opening up deep fissures. The fog signal house partly collapsed. Having been alerted by the lighthouse keeper, Trinity House arranged for a light vessel to ride off the coast as a substitute fog signal.

Rebuilding the lighthouse on higher ground cost £71,000 in 1974. Allowing for inflation, a tenfold increase in just under a hundred years seems a reasonable price. A new bungalow has been built for the keeper, who patiently explains to groups of visitors the history of the station and the changes made in recent years by technology. He points out that there is no foghorn now – ships rely on radar – and the automatic working of the lights is controlled by computer, with a panel in his bungalow that enables him to check if all is well.

If Miss Chichester could have looked into the future when she gave the headland of Morte to the National Trust in 1920, she might have been cheered to know that in less than eighty years it would be the central point of a long stretch of coast in the Trust's protection, running from west of Ilfracombe to Croyde.

A writer in 1890 saw Morte Point as 'the one unfinished corner of Devon, where the naked crags seem to quake and shiver as the winter surges boom and the winter wind whistles eerily by; whose native gauntness and grimness neither spring nor summer have the power to soften, much less tame'.[Note 2]

Such genteel shuddering away from wildness sounds laughable now, especially in bright weather with small white waves sloshing languidly around Morte Stone and Woolacombe's summer season cheerfully busy less than a mile away. But 1890 was another country. The population of Britain was little more than half what it is today; although both industrial cities and the railway network had grown fast, their capacity to obliterate open countryside was slow by comparison with that of late 20th century conurbations, trunk roads and motorways. True wildness has become hard to find, and is always under threat.

Yet on days when thick mist out of the Atlantic submerges the coast and muffles the sound of the sea, it is possible to imagine that the shoreline still lies several miles to the west, and that the wild headlands of Baggy and Morte are inland bluffs, much as they were in the days when the first human inhabitants of the far north-west corner of Devon left traces of their lives by chipping flint beach pebbles to delicate barbs for tools and weapons.

Parsons of Georgeham

Robert de Edington, 1231.

Master Oliver de Tracy, 25th April,1261.

Sir Stephen Haym, 29th September, 1272.

Edmund de Knoyle, 27th December, 1304.

Master William de Doune, 4th November, 1344.

Master John de Dyrworthe, 23rd November, 1349.

Sir Andrew de Tregors, 23rd December, 1361.

Sir John Hope, 13th December, 1374.

John Lynneley, 23rd September, 1391.

Master Martin Lercedykene, 15th July, 1422.

Master Edward Leghe, 25th April, 1433.

Sir Richard Rawe, 14th October, 1450.

William Slugge, 18th October, 1465.

Thomas Cutford, DD (no date).

John Chapelyne, 2nd September, 1499.

John Gevons, 1518.

John Holway, Canon of Exeter, 21st January, 1528. Died October, 1559.

John Greed, 1560. Buried 19th December, 1586.

William Culme, 1587. Buried 30th August, 1638, aged 90.

John Berry, 28th August, 1638. Buried 3rd February, 1649, aged 63.

William Pyke, M.A., 12th March, 1649.

Thomas Colley, 23rd May, 1661. Buried 4th June, 1698.

Carew Hoblyn, 30th July, 1698. Buried 14th March, 1728.

William Mervin, 1728.

George Drake, 11th September, 1744.

William Chichester, 7th April, 1750. Buried 6th September, 1770.

Henry Marker, 24th February, 1771. Resigned.

John Sanford, 16th December, 1771. Resigned.

Nathaniel Bridges, 17th May, 1782. Resigned.

Thomas Hole, 4th November, 1783. Buried 10th October, 1831, aged 81.

Francis Hole, 8th December, 1831. Buried 14th October, 1866.

William Chorley Loveband, 1866. Resigned. 1869.

Thomas Hole, 1869. Resigned.
Francis Hole, 29th January, 1870. Buried 10th August, 1871.
William Genn Morcom, 23rd November, 1871. Collated to Braunton.
R.B. de Wolf. 1882.
W.E. Cox, 1882.
William H.G.F. Hole, 1886 (Henry George Francis).
Walter Mathew Parker, 1914. Died 1921, aged 49.
Alfred Rose, 1922.
Algernon Edgar Worsley, 11th December, 1930.
Harry Sharples, Prebend of Exeter, 27th September, 1936.
Fisher Ferguson, M.A., Canon of Southwell, 18th November, 1957.
John Manaton, 25th June, 1959.
John Reginald Jackson, M.A., 19th May, 1967.
Bernard John Bedford Carr, 13th March, 1974.
David Kudman, B.D., 3rd October, 1988.

A brass plate on the south wall reads :
    'In loving memory of Thomas Hole, Patron of this Benefice.
Born 12th May, 1841. Died 17th May, 1889. The youngest son of
Francis Hole M.A. for 35 years rector of this parish. Through his
munificence and by the benefection of a relative, this church was
restored, AD 1876.
    He also partly built the Chapel of St. Mary Magdalene at Croyde.
This Memorial was erected by his sisters, Caroline Dene and Sarah
Jane Fursdon.'

NOTES

Chapter One

1. Keith Gardner, *Mesolithic Survey – North Devon*. TDA 89, Exeter, 1957; Revd Daniel Lysons, *Topographical and Historical Account of Devonshire'* London, 1822.
2. W.G. Hoskins, *Devon*. David and Charles, 1954.
3. *Translation of Devonshire Domesday,* Alecto Historical Editions, 1987.
4. W.G. Hoskins, op. cit.
5. A.W. Searley, *Haccombe, Part I*. TDA 50, Torquay, 1918.
6. Feet of Fines 474. Devon and Cornwall Record Society, 1912.
7. Feet of Fines 617. Devon and Cornwall Record Society.
8. Feet of Fines 1254. Devon and Cornwall Record Society.
9. Audrey M. Erskine, *The Devonshire Lay Subsidy of 1332*. Devon and Cornwall Record Society, 1969.
10. A.W. Searley *Haccombe, Part 2*. TDA 51, Tiverton, 1919.

Chapter Two

1. T.L. Stoate, *Devon Subsidy Rolls,* 1543-5. Privately printed, Bristol, 1986.
2. A.J. Howard and T.L. Stoate, *Devon Muster Roll for 1569*. Privately printed, 1977.
3. A.J. Howard and T.L. Stoate, *Devon Protestation Returns*. Privately printed, 1973.
4. T.L. Stoate, *The Devon Hearth Tax Returns*. Privately printed, Bristol, 1978.
5. Donald K. Yeoman, *Comets,* John Wiley and Sons, Inc., 1991.

Chapter Three

1. Henry Williamson, 'The Old Cob Cottage' from *The Village Book,* Cape, 1930.

Chapter Four

1. There had been a previous connection between the Chichesters and Georgeham. Lysons (*Magna Britannica,* Vol. 6, Part 2) observes that Sir Peter Carew sold Pickwell 'to Newcourt, in whose family it continued for several generations. The heiress of Toby Newcourt, the last of this family, about the middle of the 17th century, married Chichester.' The Georgeham burial register shows that 'Gregorie Chichester, Esq.' died in 1696.

Chapter Five
1. Richard Larn, *Devonshire Shipwrecks*. David and Charles, 1974.
2. *The Cave and Lundy Review,* or *Critical Revolving Light.* Barnstaple, 1824.
3. Henry Williamson, *Life in a Devon Village*. Faber, 1945.
4. A.H.A. Hamilton, TDA 11, Ilfracombe, 1879; P.F.S. Amery, TDA 24, Plymouth, 1892.

Chapter Six
1. W.H. Rogers, *Barnstaple Turnpike Trust,* TDA 74, Exeter, 1942.
2. Map of Devon published by G. and J. Cary, St. James's Street, July 2nd, 1821.
3. A.H. Slee, *Some Dead Industries of North Devon.* TDA 70, Barnstaple, 1938.
4. *Spreacombe, The Manor, Chapel and Well:* extract from MS by A.L. Barker. TDA 93, Ilfracombe, 1961, and TDA 71, 1939, Honiton.
5. Henry Williamson, *Life in a Devon Village.*

Chapter Seven
1. Paul Sanby, Devon section of *The Agricultural State of the Kingdom,* 1816. Board of Agricultural facsimile reprint. Augustus M. Kelley, New York, 1970.
2. William White, *History, Gazetteer and Directory of Devon.* 1850.

Chapter Eight
1. Benjamin Incledon, *Inscriptions from Monuments, Grave Stones and other Memorials in various churches of the County of Devon...Collected on a personal survey, in the years from 1769 to 1795.* MS in possession of North Devon Athenæum.
2. James Davidson, *Notes on North Devon Churches.*
3. *Dictionary of National Biography.*
4. Sir Stephen Glynne, 'Notes on the Churches of Devon', *Notes and Queries,* London, 1933.
5. William White, *History, Gazetteer and Directory of Devon,* 1878/9

Chapter Nine
No notes.

Chapter Ten
1. There were four sisters in all: Edith, Lucy, Margaret and Winifred. The first three were all painters in oils and water colours who quite often exhibited at the Royal Academy. Lucy's work first appeared

there in 1895, Edith's in 1898 and Margaret's in 1903. *Royal Academy of Arts:* Exhibitors 1880-1970.

The subjects of Margaret Kemp-Welch's murals in Georgeham church were The Annunciation, St. George slaying the dragon and St. Francis of Assisi. She spent the later part of her life in Throwleigh, and died in 1968.

Chapter Eleven
1. R.W. Thompson, *The Pink House in Angel Street.* Dennis Dobson, 1954.

Chapter Twelve
1. Inkerman Rogers. TDA 62, Princetown, 1930.
2. Revd Daniel Lysons, op. cit.
3. S.E. Ellacott, *Braunton Ships and Seaman.* Quest Publications, 1980.
4. Anonymous, but probably written by the Revd George Tugwell, author of *A Guide to Ilfracombe and the Neighbouring Towns.*
5. J.L.W. Page, *The Coasts of Devon and Lundy Island,* London, 1895. Two other writers who mentioned the chapel were the anonymous author of a *Handbook for Travellers,* published by John Murray in 1865, and R.N. Worth, whose *Tourists' Guide to North Devon* was published in 1886.
6. H.M. Tomlinson, *Old Junk.* Jonathan Cape, 1925 (2nd Edition).

Chapter Thirteen
1. S.E. Ellacott, *Braunton Farms and Farmers.* Aycliffe Press, 1981.
2. Bridget Cherry and Nikolaus Pevsner, *The Buildings of England: Devon.* Penguin Books, 2nd edition, 1989.
3. Arthur H. Slee, *This Devon of Ours,* Barnstaple, no date.
4. C.S. Ward, *North Devon and North Cornwall.* Thorough Guides. Thomas Nelson and Sons, 1908.
5. R.N. Worth, op. cit.
6. *A Book of the South West.* Printed for the 75th Annual Meeting of the British Medical Association. Exeter, 1907.
7. Henry Williamson, *The Pathway,* Jonathan Cape, 1928.

Chapter Fourteen
1. Bill Foster. *Braunton Great Field and Marshes Trail.* Braunton Conservation Project, 1986.
2. In July, 1994, the *Western Morning News* reported that a management study of the Great Field had been carried out by the Exeter Archæological Field Unit; it was hoped that the field might be

designated a conservation area and that grants for its protection might be obtained from the Countryside Commission's Countryside Stewardship Programme.
3. Henry Williamson, *The Lone Swallows,* 2nd Edition. Putnam, 1933.

Chapter Fifteen
1. Pevsner, op. cit.
2. William White, 1850. op. cit.
3. Richard Larn, op. cit.
4. William White's *Directory of Devon,* 1878/9.
5. Kelly's *Directory of Devon,* 1883.
6. C.G. Harper, *The North Devon Coast.* Chapman and Hall, 1908.
7. *Guide to Bideford, Ilfracombe and North-West Devon,* Ward Lock, London, 1905/6.

Chapter Sixteen
1. Lieut. H.M. Denham, R.N. *Remarks and Sailing Directions relative to Lundy Island and the North Coast of Devonshire.'* Published by Nathaniel V. Lee and Capt. G.F. Herbert, R.N. Liverpool, 1832.
2. R.N. Worth, op. cit.

Index

Folkestone, 61
Forda, (Ford), 9, 18, 43, 44, 71
Forda House, 72
Fort Hill, Barnstaple, 71
Fortescue Arms, 123
Fortescue family, 39, 55, 66
Fortescue, Earl, 35, 49, 71
Fortescue, fourth Earl, 66
Foulkes, Cedric, 74
Fox, Robert, 55
France, 11, 12, 34, 61, 62
Fraser, Robert, 20
Fremington, 20

G
Gammon and Son, 124
Gammon, John, 52
Gammon, Richard, 123, 124
Gauntel, William, 9
General View of the County of Devon,
20
George and Catherine, lifeboat, 85
George V, 127
Georgeham, 2, 4, 5, 7, 9, 11, 12, 13,
14, 16, 19, 20, 21, 24, 34, 35, 36, 39
Georgeham and Croyde Rifle Club, 71
Georgeham church, 6, 69
Georgeham school, 45
Gilbert, W.S., 33
Glynne, Sir Stephen, 54
Goff, Virginia, 113
Golding, Nancy, 31
Goldsberry, Captain, 34
Gordon Lodge, Woolacombe, 124
Gosse, Philip, 120
Gould, R.D., 119
Gould, Simon, 55
Gower, The, South Wales, 131
Grace Woodbury, lifeboat, 122

Grantham, 61
Gratton, 7
Great Field, Braunton, 102
Great North Road, 38
Great War see First World War
Great Western, 126
Grey, Capt the Hon Henry, 31, 33
Grey, William, 33
Gryffyrd, Thomas, 9

H
Halford, Warwickshire, 120
Hall, Townsend, 1, 93
Halley's Comet, 14
Halley, Edmond, 14
Halsinger Bog, 102
Ham Revel, 20, 21
Ham town, (Georgeham), 19
Ham, (Georgeham), 12
Hamme, 5, 8
Hancock, Dorothy, 18
Hannaborough Lane, 109
Harper, Nicholas, 13
Harris family, 10, 14
Harris, John, of Pickwell, 18, 19
Harris, Miss Mary Ann, 56
Harry, John, 13
Hartland, 83, 85, 111
Hartland Abbey, 35
Hartland Point, 30
Hartley, Mary, 86, 120
Harvey, Professor Leslie, 101, 103,
Hawthornden Prize for Literature, 65
Hayme, Sir Stephen, 7
Heanton Punchardon, 33, 39, 102
Heathercombe Hotel, 115
Heddon, 18
Heddon Mill, 74
Heinkel, 78

Henry VIII, 11, 12
Hernaman, Farmer, 85
Heygate, John, later Sir John, 65
Hibbert, Charles, 64
Hibbert, Ida Loetitia, 62
Hill, Sergeant John, 35, 36
History of the British Army, 66
Hoblyn, Revd Carew, 16, 19, 24
Holcote, Thomas, 44
Hole Cleave, 44
Hole family, 21
Hole Lane, 109
Hole Mill, 18, 44
Hole, Anne, 25
Hole, Frances, 58
Hole, Mary Brooking, 55
Hole, Rev Francis, (1870 - 1871), 21
Hole, Revd Francis, 21, 22, 36, 39, 49
Hole, Revd Thomas, 20, 22, 34, 39, 56
Hole, Thomas, 21, 54
Hole, W.H.G.F., 21
Hole, William Henry George Francis, 21
Holland, 112
Holway, John, Canon of Exeter, 12
Holwill, James, 52
Home Guard, 82
Home in Ham, 76, 77, 78
Horden, Captain, 34
Horsey Island, 112
Howard, Richard, 56
Hustwayte, Herbert Leonard, 90
Hyde, Edwin, 113
Hyde, Miss Connie, 113
Hyde, Miss Florence, 67, 113

I

Idonea, daughter of Robert de Pidikwill, 7

Ilfracombe, 8, 33, 34, 35, 39, 40, 51, 52, 67, 79, 85, 98, 117, 120, 122, 123, 126, 131
Ilfracombe Battalion of the Home Guard, 82
Ilfracombe Beds, (Devonian Period), 128
Ilfracombe Hotel, 79
Image, Selwyn, 119
Incledon House, 36
Incledon, A.W., R.A.M.C, 59
Incledon, Benjamin, 53
Instow, 93, 103
Ireland, 112
Iron Age, 2
Isca Dumnoniorum, 2

J

Jack-a-Jack, lifeboat, 122
Jefferies, Richard, 61
Jeremy, Mr & Mrs George, 85
John the Baptist, 42
Journal of the National Life-boat Institution, 86
Junkers 88, 78

K

Kelly's Directory, 71
Kemp-Welch, Margaret, 66, 72
Kennel Field, Georgeham, 22
Kent, 98
Kentisbury Cottage, 77
Kidman, William, of Huntington, 33
King Stephen, 119
Kings Arms, Georgeham, 43, 49, 62, 69, 113
Kingston-on-Thames, 14
Kittiwell, Croyde, 44, 67
Knaresborough, 118

P

Paddington, 126
Paris, 14
Passchendaele, 61
Patmos, island of, 89
Pearce, Richard, 58
Peninsular War, 36
Peren, Thomas, 13
Petherham, Mrs Mary, 124
Petherick, Charles, 99
Petherick, Hester, 99
Pevsner, Nikolaus, 126
Pickwell, 4, 5, 6, 7, 8, 9, 11, 14, 42, 49, 109
Pickwell chapel, 55
Pickwell Down, 74
Pickwell Down Beds, (Devonian Period), 128
Pickwell Manor, 67, 71
Pigot and Co, *National Commercial Directory*, 51
Plymouth, 40, 81, 85
Poor Law, 47
Portland, Duke of, 35
Portrait of a Patriot, 77
Potter's Hill, Woolacombe, 127
Prince Regent, 49
Putsborough, 10, 19, 30, 36, 52, 78, 115
Putsborough Manor, 45

Q

Quival, Bishop Peter, 7

R

RAF Chivenor, 102, 108
Reed, William, 52
Reinald, 6
Restoration, of Charles II, 14

Richards, John, 20, 56
Ring o' Bells, Georgeham, 49
Risdon, Tristram, 8, 37, 88, 91
RNLI, 85, 86, 122
Roadway Farm, near Georgeham, 74
Robert and Catherine, lifeboat, 85
Rock House (Rock Inn), Georgeham, 49, 62
Rock, William, 124
Rockham Bay, Morthoe, 120
Rockham Villas, Woolacombe, 124
Rockley House, Woolacombe, 123
Rodd, Thomas, 85
Rogers Webber, Philip, 35
Rolle, Henry, 18
Roman legions, 2
Rome, 118
Rose, Mrs, 69
Rose, Revd Alfred, 67
Royal Aeronautical Establishment, 79
Royal Albert Museum, 2
Ruddock and Sons, Messrs, 55
Rumpet, near Croyde, 44
Russell, Dr, 49
Rynchosinopsis Wrightii, 101

S

Sabrina, (the river Severn), 2
Sailing Directions for Lundy and the North Coast of Devon, 129
St Agnes, 89
St Albino, (St Aubyn) 6
St Anne, 89
St Anne's Chapel, 40, 88, 107
St Anthony, 20
St Aubyn family, 6
St Aubyn, Guy, 6
St Aubyn, Isabel, 6, 8, 9
St Aubyn, Ivan, 9

READERS NOTES